EXPECT
TO WIN

EXPECT TO WIN

10 PROVEN STRATEGIES
for THRIVING *in the* WORKPLACE

CARLA A. HARRIS

HUDSON
STREET
PRESS

HUDSON STREET PRESS
Published by Penguin Group
Penguin Group (USA) Inc., 375 Hudson Street, New York, New York 10014, U.S.A. • Penguin
Group (Canada), 90 Eglinton Avenue East, Suite 700, Toronto, Ontario, Canada M4P 2Y3
(a division of Pearson Penguin Canada Inc.) • Penguin Books Ltd, 80 Strand, London
WC2R 0RL, England • Penguin Ireland, 25 St. Stephen's Green, Dublin 2, Ireland (a division of
Penguin Books Ltd.) • Penguin Group (Australia), 250 Camberwell Road, Camberwell,
Victoria 3124, Australia (a division of Pearson Australia Group Pty. Ltd.) • Penguin Books
India Pvt. Ltd., 11 Community Centre, Panchsheel Park, New Delhi – 110 017,
India • Penguin Group (NZ), 67 Apollo Drive, Rosedale, North Shore 0632, New Zealand
(a division of Pearson New Zealand Ltd.) • Penguin Books (South Africa) (Pty.) Ltd., 24
Sturdee Avenue, Rosebank, Johannesburg 2196, South Africa

Penguin Books Ltd., Registered Offices: 80 Strand, London WC2R 0RL, England

First published by Hudson Street Press, a member of Penguin Group (USA) Inc.

First Printing, February 2009
10   9   8   7   6   5   4   3

REGISTERED TRADEMARK—MARCA REGISTRADA
HUDSON
STREET
PRESS

LIBRARY OF CONGRESS CATALOGING-IN-PUBLICATION DATA
Harris, Carla A.
   Expect to win : proven strategies for success from a Wall Street vet / Carla A. Harris.
      p. cm.
   ISBN 978-1-59463-051-4 (alk. paper)
   1. Success in business.   2. Career development.   I. Title.
   HF5386.H2726 2009
   650.1—dc22   2008030347

Printed in the United States of America
Set in Bembo

PUBLISHER'S NOTE

This book is printed on acid-free paper. ∞

This book is dedicated to my mother, Billie Joyce Harris my role model extraordinaire. I will always love you.

Contents

Introduction

When I began my career on Wall Street in 1987, right out of Harvard Business School, there was no playbook. There was no one, especially no one of color, I was particularly close to who could teach me how to be successful in this high stakes, high-strung environment. I had bought into the idea of a pure meritocracy, 100 percent objectivity, and thought that merely being smart and hardworking would be my keys to long-term success. Wrong! What I failed to understand is that despite the fact that the financial services industry, investment banking in particular, is a numbers-oriented, bottom-line driven business, it is not 100 percent objective, and objectivity is at the core of meritocracy.

After more than two decades working as a woman in the intense, dynamic, competitive, tough environment called Wall Street, I have learned that Wall Street (every industry, really) is driven by people, and people are subjective by nature. Therefore, most environments are not true meritocracies. Hard work and smarts are not enough to succeed. For the success equation to be complete, hard work, skills, and intelligence need a few more additives, such as strategy, relationships, politics, tenacity, and faith.

This equation is the key to long-term success in finance and almost any other industry, including medicine, law, entertainment, publishing, and even academia. As I travel around giving speeches at various business schools, colleges, universities, corporations, and professional symposiums, inevitably people will ask the same types of questions about navigating their career. These "pearls" (as I would eventually call them) of knowledge and wisdom I have gathered over my almost twenty-one years on the street hold many of the answers.

I often say that these pearls have been battle tested because I acquired most of them by making mistakes and then figuring out a way to correct them, usually realizing after the fact what I should have done to affect a better, easier, or different outcome. I have tested and retested these pearls over and over again, eventually learning to strategize before the fact and then watching my goal transpire as planned. They continue to work for me today, as they work for others who have employed them.

While much of today's "how to succeed in business" literature promotes the necessity of having a mentor and planning for one's success, I have found that most professionals, particularly in the early to mid stages of their careers, still do not have practical, strategic tools that they can employ to help them reach their career goals. Whether it's at the beginning of their career, or when they need to change careers or assignments, or whether they are looking to redirect or reenergize their career, most professionals have no plan or tools to support them.

While most people walk into their careers with some background knowledge from undergraduate or graduate school or previous experience, most of us do not have the tools or experience to successfully navigate the political environment or know what we need to do to proactively take control of our careers. In fact, most people don't realize that they are responsible for actively and aggressively managing their careers. Most people think that they need only keep their heads down, work hard, work smart, and everything falls into place for success. We are told that we need to have a mentor, but no one tells you how to find that mentor, what to look for in a *really good* mentor, or how to use one when you find one. Nor are we told that while a mentor is important, a sponsor is the most important relationship that you need in order to move through and upward within an organization.

When our career moves sideways or gets off track, no one tells you how to manage your relationships to get back on track or exactly what to say when you go to your boss to have that critical conversation about repositioning yourself within your department or within the firm. What *exactly* do you? How do you recover from a major mistake? How do you keep it from sinking your career, and what conversation do you have with your boss?

When I was having some tough times in the beginning of my career, particularly in the make or break middle portion, I would go and talk to people I considered mentors. Instead of getting step-by-step advice on how to navigate, manage, and succeed in the situation, often I received advice like "You should find another area to work in, because it doesn't seem like this one is heading in the right direction," or "You should try to get different assignments," or "I wouldn't accept that assignment if I were you." While some of that may have been useful advice, no one told me *how* to approach my boss, or *exactly what to say* in order to be effective and achieve my objectives.

There is nothing more frustrating than gathering up the courage to ask for help and then receiving generalized, nonspecific, blanket advice. It leaves you feeling more frustrated, helpless, and scared. I know that's how I felt. While I was quite smart, having these types of conversations was new territory for me, as it is for many people. Having the tools to have the conversations effectively, especially the first time, is essential, because you often only get one chance at it.

As I began to figure out "the game," the strategies, the language, the timing for success in business—the key survival tools—I vowed that when I became senior and when people came to me for advice, I would give them specific, play-by-play answers about what they needed to do. I wanted to not only give them strategies; I also wanted to help to identify and confirm the problem, and even help to fashion the dialogue, behavior, and execution to help them solve whatever issue they might have.

I wanted anyone who had the courage to come to me for help to walk away from our meeting feeling satisfied. I wanted them to feel that they now had the solution to their problem, or at least to feel good about seeking help, advice, or just a conversation to remove what was impeding their ability to maximize their potential.

The truth is that I began sharing the pearls I had learned long before I became a senior executive. I was sharing them broadly after only three years in the business. This is the essence of *Expect to Win*. The pearls are the hard-earned lessons that I have acquired after twenty years on Wall Street. Each chapter will share my views and expertise in the various areas that contribute to career success. Or, conversely, if you are not careful, areas that can derail a career. And at the end of every chapter I'll include at least five of Carla's Pearls. These are takeaways that you can remember and apply on the job; you might even want to copy them down and pin them to your computer monitor or bulletin board or carry them in your portfolio or wallet to remind you how to navigate the day-to-day complexities and challenges of the workplace.

I want to share these lessons with women, women of color, and anyone (men, too) who desires to maximize their potential and claim their power in any professional environment. Power lies within each of us, no matter what your job, your gender, or your skin color. And if you recognize, harness, and use your power properly, it can become one of the key drivers in your career.

This book is for anyone who wants to claim that power and use it to expand not only their own life but the lives of others. *Expect to Win* is for anyone looking for the tools to help them handle the common challenges we all face at some point in our careers, anyone who wants to triumph over those challenges, successfully go forward in their careers, reach their goals, and expect to win.

EXPECT
TO WIN

CHAPTER 1

AUTHENTICITY
The Power Is You

There is only one *you!*
The day your company hired you, someone else did *not* get the job because *you* were the best candidate. They hired you because you had the best combination of skills, personality, and potential and a unique blend of values and abilities. Over any other person they interviewed, the company felt that you could best execute the job, fulfill their need for talent, and satisfy their specific need for a discrete skill set. You got the job because you had a competitive advantage over all of the other candidates. That important competitive advantage? *You.* No one else can be you the way you can; this is your source of power within the organization.

One of the keys to your long-term success in any organization is to own the person who you *really* are. If you bring that original, best you to work every day, the one that interviewed for and got the job, then you can maintain your competitive advantage in the organization now and, more importantly, over time.

Bringing the real you to work allows you to be free! Free to learn new concepts, free to be creative and responsive, free to take risks—all of which helps to enhance the professional that you are and makes you valuable to the organization. In today's competitive environment, the person who learns new concepts quickly, who can adapt commercially, or, in other words, can apply those lessons in a way that can make money for the firm, and who is also client-oriented, is the person who moves most quickly in a company and is most handsomely rewarded.

If you are preoccupied with trying to play a role or trying to behave, speak, or act the way you *think* others want you to, your mind won't be free to perform at your highest level, be flexible, and be able to adapt to changes. Putting on an act eventually becomes exhausting and uses up valuable mental capacity that could instead be directed toward making important contributions at work.

The reason that I am such a strong advocate for being who you really are at work is that doing so gives you confidence. When you are comfortable with who you are, you exude confidence, and that's attractive to clients and to colleagues. Others want to listen to confident people; they want to hear your ideas, they trust your judgment, and they will buy what you are selling, whether it is a product, a financing pitch, or a decision.

When you are not being who you really are, at some point you will begin to appear uncomfortable to others. Especially in client-facing businesses, such as investment banking or sales, trust in relationships is an important element of success. When you act and speak with confidence, it contributes to your performance. If you appear to be tentative or apprehensive (which usually happens when you are lacking confidence), then you open the door for your clients to doubt what you are saying, you potentially lose the opportunity to win the business, and you open the door for a competitor to get the upper hand in a relationship.

A lack of confidence can also hurt in your internal interactions as well. When you are confident with who you are, it helps you to build trust in relationships with the people you work with. Especially if your work environment is very competitive or has a relatively flat hierarchy, which also tends to intensify internal competition, then it is imperative that you have confidence in who you are and what you are doing. If you are in a competitive environment where the rule is "up or out" (either you move up within the organization over a period of time or you have to leave the organization) and your colleagues realize that you are not comfortable with who you are or in your work, then they will actively try to find ways to make you doubt yourself.

If you are constantly questioning your abilities in the workplace, then sooner or later your boss is likely to notice and their trust or belief in you will be impaired. And when your boss starts to doubt whether or not you can do the work or have the ability to sell your ideas, then you are very likely to be viewed as someone who cannot or should not move up within the organization or get the opportunity to have bigger or better clients or other responsibilities.

We all have strengths and weaknesses, gifts and talents. Have the confidence to play up yours. Be proud about what you do well and who you are. And work to improve your weaknesses whenever possible. You don't have to wear either on your sleeve, but don't suppress what's good and interesting about yourself either.

Putting on an act eventually will manifest itself into appearing discontent, and if it's at a really inopportune moment, such as when you're presenting to an important client, it could cost you a piece of business, a new assignment, or a promotion. And if clients or colleagues feel they don't know who you are, that you will lean any way the wind blows, they won't fully trust you. When that happens, you have created a competitive disadvantage for yourself compared to the colleague who is confident, stands by their word, and knows who they are.

KNOW WHO YOU ARE

So how do you know who you are? It seems like an easy question, but many people have never really taken the time to think about it. If you haven't, you need to ask yourself some important questions: What are your key strengths and weaknesses? Why are you in the profession that you are in? Why did you choose the firm that you chose? What are your goals at the firm, in that department, and for the specific job or seat that you are in?

You get to know who you are not only by asking these questions, but also by the experiences you have and by paying close attention to how you react in different situations and understanding why you are doing what you are doing. When you are comfortable with the decisions that *you* make and why you make them, then you are starting to get a handle on who you really are. Further, knowing who you are helps you to quickly identify when things go awry or when your career is veering off track, and it helps you to quickly identify solutions to remedy challenging situations. If you know who you are in an environment, where you belong, and how you fit in, then you will have the confidence to make changes or to speak up as needed to make sure that you are maximizing your success.

In order to stay focused on remaining authentic and being the best original you can be, you must first understand what your competitive strengths are and concentrate on improving your weaknesses. In any situation, you always want to both lead with your strengths and commit to making time to improve those skills that you think you need to work on. At all times, you must be able to explain why *you* belong in a particular position, why *you* deserve a promotion, why *you* deserve the raise or the highest tier of bonuses, or simply why *you* are so good at what you do.

Focusing on these questions will help you develop that all-important "elevator speech." That's the quick speech you need to have at the ready at all times; the one that explains to people who you are and what you want in the time it takes to go up or down the elevator. This is an important skill to develop. You never know when or where you will have the opportunity to talk to someone about your strengths and goals within a company. Therefore, you need to be clear about *you*, your goals, and your assets, and have your elevator speech about yourself ready to use at any time. Your power lies in putting your best self forward every day. If you are always focused on presenting your authentic self wherever you go, you will be able to automatically present a speech about yourself whenever the situation demands it, and you'll be able to do so in a compelling and convincing manner.

The people who seem comfortable in their own skin and who are bringing their real selves to work generally also are the same people who can have an honest dialogue with their bosses, who have the courage to ask for the promotion, the bonus, or the new assignment, and who are quick to point out when someone or something is impeding their success. On the other hand, those who have submerged who they truly are, or, worse, have completely lost sight of who they are, are the people who typically are passive about their career, generally unhappy, and under the illusion that things will just happen for them without any effort on their part. These people generally don't own their decisions, their positions, their career trajectory (the direction your career will take), or themselves. They are not the first to be thought of for new assignments or promotions. Their careers tend to stall and they are left behind.

Consider Peter, who outside of the office is a very charismatic guy. He is affable and comfortable with who he is; he loves to debate, and is extremely articulate. He builds relationships easily and loves to connect people in his network. He is also recognized as a "braniac" among his peers because of his outstanding analytical and structuring skills. At work, however, Peter is a completely different person. He is quiet and in meetings often only speaks after everyone else has spoken. He never leads a discussion unless pushed by his boss and he has never articulated in a concrete, compelling manner what he wants from the organization or what he wants out of his career. He is afraid of rocking the boat.

Peter often develops creative financing ideas and shares them with peers, but he never steps up to take credit for or be recognized for his contribution, instead allowing his ideas to be integrated with those of others. Peter has been at his firm for eighteen years and has not had a promotion in more than eight years. Even though he does excellent work, he is not perceived as someone who can penetrate client thought, make and close a sale, or be solely responsible for generating revenue. He is not perceived as a leader; a solid citizen, yes, but not a leader.

There is a distinct difference between inside-the-office Peter and outside-the-office Peter, and unfortunately that difference is costing Peter in his career. The outside Peter is an influential thought leader. He makes compelling arguments and leads people to his way of thinking. Yet he does not bring that Peter to work with him every day. He is not his authentic self in the work environment, and as a result his career has stalled. If he would exercise his voice, leverage his outstanding structuring skills, and sell them internally, he would move quickly within the organization. He clearly cares about his work, but he hasn't approached his boss and outlined what he wants from his career, from the organization, and how he can get there. Since he has submerged that part of who he is, he is not realizing *his* full value in the organization professionally or economically.

Owning who you are really are will give you the confidence

to speak up for yourself if you think you are not being treated fairly or not being properly recognized for who you are and your contributions to the organization. I often find that people who think that the organization is not recognizing their contributions, are in fact not really exhibiting the skills, strengths, or traits that they *think* they are. Before you start to blame the organization for not seeing what you offer, ask yourself, Am I showing them that I can penetrate or influence client thought? That I can win client business? That I care about being promoted? Or am I assuming that the organization should know this or observe this on its own? Am I bringing my contributions to the table in a visible and compelling way?"

AUTHENTICITY TRANSCENDS THE PERSONALITY

When I say to bring your authentic self to work, I am not saying that if you like wearing jeans and T-shirts and the code of attire at your workplace is conservative button-down suits that you should come to the office wearing your casual attire. Part of being authentic is choosing a job and an environment that you are comfortable working in, one where you know that you can comply with both the written and unwritten rules.

Consider the code of attire within financial services. The common code of attire at all of the big brokerage houses is expensive, conservative suits, shoes, scarves, ties, and so on for both men and women. While still largely the same, things have relaxed a bit in recent times with the introduction of casual business attire. When I made the decision that financial services was the industry I wanted to pursue a career in and an environment that I wanted to work in, I asked myself whether I was willing to put on that uniform every day. Did I understand the financial commitment that I would be making to my wardrobe to play in this game? Yes! It was part of the territory, and it was a territory that I wanted to do business in. It was also consistent with who I am. I like nice clothes and in most cases I am more of a conservative dresser than not, so it was easy for me to do. I do not feel like I am getting up every morning and putting on a different Carla, somebody who I am not. I may not dress this way on the weekends or at parties, but I did want to work in an environment where this type of uniform was required every day.

Every industry has a code of conduct, including attire, a persona for its professionals. There are expectations for how you should behave or what your predominant skill set or perspective should be. For example, a banker is expected to have strong quantitative skills; a trader should be able to spot money-making opportunities quickly, to be nimble and a quick decision maker; a lawyer is expected to have great oratorical skills; and a consultant should have outstanding analytical skills. When considering the right seat for you, you have to ask yourself whether these expectations are credible and easy for you to satisfy.

The expectations of an industry or position have to be consistent with who you are on a fundamental level. If you think it will be a struggle for you to meet them, then you should seriously consider whether or not that profession, career, or job is the right one for you. In other words, if you are a quiet, introspective thinker with creative skills who hates to make presentations and prefers to work alone, then working as part of a sales team at a pharmaceutical company probably is not the right job for you. Conversely, if you are an analytical thinker who loves to crunch numbers and analyze deals, you probably wouldn't do well working in the creative department of an advertising firm.

Life is way too short to walk into a job every day feeling like you are not operating at 150 percent and excited about doing a great job. If you are resenting your environment or your job, then your authentic self will get lost in that company, as will your competitive advantage. Further, it's likely that your career trajectory will stall and not move upward, or, worse, will head downward.

If this is the case for you, if you find yourself unenthusiastic about your job or career, stop and ask yourself what would change things. Figure out what you need to help you to feel good about walking in the front door of your office building every morning. What would have to happen for you to want to spend eight to twelve hours in the same place every day? Consider your strengths—the ones that got you hired in the first place—as well as your weaknesses. Do you have an opportunity to showcase those key strengths every day? To leverage them? To use them to build value for your company? Are you getting an opportunity to improve your weaknesses and to add to your skill/experience tool chest? If the answer to any of these questions is no, maybe all you need is to seek out a little training. But you also have to be truthful with yourself and consider whether perhaps you are in the wrong seat, in the wrong department, at the wrong firm, or even in the wrong industry.

I'M STRUGGLING UP THE LADDER BUT IT'S LEANING AGAINST THE WRONG BUILDING

A question that I often get at the end of my speeches is, "Suppose I have taken a good look at myself and my organization and I see now that I cannot really be my authentic self at work. There is a clear mismatch between the types of things that inspire or excite me and what the organization is looking for in its model for success. What do I do?" Let's say you've read through this chapter and you've done exactly as I suggested. You've sat down and made out your list of strengths and weaknesses. You've reviewed your firm's Web site and marketing literature and feel you understand what the company thinks is important. And then you realize that your worst fears are confirmed, that you are working in the wrong type of job or industry! You've suspected it all along, you've never really felt comfortable in your job or at industry events, but now you see it on paper. How do you change it or get out of it? Is it too late for you?

Let me assure you, it isn't too late. But I won't lie to you either. The further you are into your career, the more challenging it may be to remedy the situation. But you have to understand that if you stay, you will never be valued or rewarded in a substantial way or one that makes you feel accomplished and successful in your career. Why? Because you won't offer your very best self to the organization. That nagging voice inside saying, "You should be working somewhere else" will never go away, not fully. You constantly will wonder whether if you were doing something else you would be making more money. Would you be happier? If you are not planning to retire in the next year, then you still have time to change the situation so you can be more productive and happier in your professional life.

Here's an example of someone who did just that. Anne worked as a writer in financial services marketing and communications for nearly seventeen years. While she enjoyed writing brochures and white papers and creating Web site copy, she was never really passionate about the investment topics she wrote about. She did well enough in her career but never really felt like she belonged in the Wall Street environment, sensing that her laid-back, creative, introspective personality didn't fit with her hard-driving, intense colleagues. Her reviews were always good, people liked her, and she had a reputation as an excellent writer, but she longed to write about topics she felt a personal connection to.

During her free time, Anne volunteered for several nonprofits and would often write articles about the people she met while doing community work. She also loved to write about spiritual or women's issues just for fun. Anne noticed that her spirit came alive when working on these types of stories, and she often would work late into the night to finish them and never felt tired. She was passionate about getting these articles published, while conversely, writing about stocks and investment products in her day job left her feeling bored.

Having reached the VP level and senior writer status, Anne knew she had no interest in pursuing the next logical step in her career progression, to head of marketing and communications. She knew it was time for a change. She spent some time thinking and got honest about who she was, what kind of environment she was best suited to, and what kind of things she liked to do. While she enjoyed the salary and other benefits she earned working in financial services, her focus and passions had changed over the years. Things like flexible work hours in a less structured setting and the opportunity to immerse herself in topics she cared about, such as spirituality, personal empowerment, and people doing good works in the world were more important to her. So, while continuing to work full time, for three and a half years Anne returned to school, taking classes in the evenings and earning her master's in journalism. Also during that three and a half years she looked for every opportunity she could find to network with magazine and book publishers, editors, and other writers, inviting people to informational lunches, attending seminars and speeches, and scouring the Internet for information about various writing careers. And just before finishing her degree, while attending a networking event hosted at her own Wall Street firm, she met an author who needed a ghostwriter for a spiritual book. She jumped at the chance and eventually left her job in financial services. She is now happy and fulfilled earning her living working as a free-lance writer and editor.

Of course we all have economic concerns and most of us work because we have to—few of us are independently wealthy! But if this example speaks to you, when you took the job, like Anne, on some level you likely knew that it wasn't right for you. You took it just to have a job, and as a result, you gave away your real power. I don't say this to beat up on you. But, like Anne, it's time to take back your power. If you are doing a job that you love do-ing, you will excel, and if you excel, the money, the opportunity, and the power will follow. This is not to say that your only option is to leave your company or completely change industries. Com-mit to spending the next twelve to twenty-four months thinking about what you want out of your career. Ask yourself what you are good at. Even if you are just starting out at twenty-two or twenty-three years old, you know what things you like to do. Or ask yourself what you want to learn how to do. What skills or experiences would you like to add to your personal platform? Once you answer those questions, then ask yourself what you can get out of this organization. What does it offer you? Does it offer the chance to learn selling skills? Quantitative skills? What can you learn and use so that you can then go and sell it to someone else at a higher price in a different job, in a different department, or for another company or industry. Choosing a career just for the money is not a prerequisite for long-term success. Figuring this out and then developing or enhancing new or transferable skills should now be your focus. It is what you will use as a launching pad for the next step in your career.

On most days you should be able to make the case that you are adding value to your firm, taking steps toward realizing your per-sonal goals, and that you are enjoying doing it. If you aren't, you need to reevaluate where you are and exercise the courage to do something to change it. Otherwise you will continue operating at a competitive disadvantage, and doing so over a long period of time eventually will cause you and your career to falter.

KNOW YOUR GOALS

You don't walk into a job, a company, or a career thinking that you are going to change it, unless you are being hired to do just that. This is not to say that you can't make changes—maybe you can—but you have to first ask yourself whether you are comfortable operating in it as it is. Maybe you are not planning to be in that career or profession long term. Perhaps you are doing it for a short period of time, using it as a stepping stone to something else, or for the money, or for the exposure. That is a perfectly good plan, but own it and commit to be your best self while you are there, because you are there as part of your plan. That is how to be authentic.

Authenticity really begins before you walk through the front door to a new job, career, or assignment. It calls for you to understand what your goals are in the assignment before you begin. You must be able to answer questions such as, Why am I taking on this assignment? Does this assignment/project make sense because of the people I will be exposed to or the skills I will acquire? Is this assignment right for me because it furthers my objectives? These are all key questions to make sure you have aligned what you are doing with who you really are. Knowing why you are doing something in the workplace will keep you aligned authentically and, as we discussed before, will give you the opportunity to have the freedom to really learn, create, and add value to your work environment.

KEEP AN EYE ON YOUR AUTHENTIC SELF

When I've had difficulties in my career, it generally has been when I had lost sight of who I really am or of what my goals were. It was those times when powerful Carla, who easily speaks her mind, was not present, and fearful, unsure Carla was at the table.

I remember when I was just starting out in my career and was considered a junior person. I would worry that being who I was wouldn't be accepted. I thought that I had to do things exactly the way I saw my colleagues or other senior people do them. Now anyone who knows me even just a little bit knows that I am an honest person who speaks the truth. You can always count on me to be a straight shooter. I am not afraid to speak in an open environment. But back then I was concerned that if I spoke up in the way that felt most comfortable for me and shared my ideas with the senior people in the room, especially my bosses, or even the clients, that people would think I had stepped out of line or that I was not expressing myself in a compelling way. I also was afraid that if I went too far out on a limb with a thought or an idea that the senior people in the room might not support me and back me up. After all, what if I said the wrong thing or made a mistake? They might just leave me hanging there, flapping in the wind. Rather than risk offending or losing a client or receiving internal criticism, I would sit in meetings and not contribute. I would diligently prepare for the meeting beforehand, but then I would get there and just sit, never saying a word!

Then I learned through the grapevine that a well-respected, high-ranking woman at the firm had said, "She doesn't say anything in meetings; I don't know if she's smart or if she's stupid." She was talking about me! (For more on speaking up, see Chapter 6.)

Instead of helping me, as I thought being quiet and not sharing the real me would, it hurt me! The perception of me was not a good one. Instead of seeing me as the smart, capable Carla that I was, the perception of me was: "What's wrong with her? Why doesn't she speak? Does she know what is going on? Is she following the discussion? Does she even have a clue?"

I realized that as long as I sat playing it safe in silence, that no one would ever know who I was or what I was capable of. It soon became very clear that if I wanted to be successful in my career and considered an important member of the team and the organization, I couldn't allow fear to keep me quiet any longer. The authentic Carla was not fearful, and she certainly wasn't shy or quiet. Somewhere along the way I lost my voice, I submerged the real me, as I was trying to be what I *thought* would equate with success in the environment.

FOCUS ON THE RIGHT THINGS

Even after I started to speak up in meetings, I still can remember making several presentations to clients that did not go well. Why? Because I was trying to present in a way that I thought would be acceptable to my colleagues and was considering the client *second*. I would spend long hours going over information, making sure that I covered all of the important points, making sure that I would sound impressive to my colleagues rather than focusing on impressing my client. I wanted to make sure that if we lost the presentation my coworkers couldn't say that I did not know all of the important characteristics of my product or that I did not present it the way *they* would have presented it. With my colleagues as my focus rather than my clients, while my presentations were organized and articulate, unfortunately they also were flat and less than compelling. In fact, the feedback from my colleagues on those early presentations was that I sounded rote. They said I would just barrel through the facts and had no personality. By trying so hard to give a presentation in somebody else's style, not only did I fail to impress my colleagues (the wrong objective anyway), but I also failed to connect with the client. I was so preoccupied with worrying about what my colleagues would think of me and what I said that I couldn't focus on bringing my best self to the meeting. Rather than focusing on *my* strategy of effectively communicating *my* message, building a rapport and laying a foundation for a relationship with the client, I was too worried about what *they* (my colleagues) would think of my presentation, how *they* would perceive my interaction with my client, and how *they* would portray it back to the organization. Because I was not focused on the unique competitive advantage that is *me*, consequently I did not effectively communicate why I was the best at what I do and why my firm was the best the client would ever find to handle the deal. The result? I didn't show the real Carla, I didn't show my best self, and the client didn't hear the most excellent ideas and what I had to contribute. I did not effectively sell myself or my organization.

After repeatedly having this experience and hearing the same less-than-enthusiastic feedback, I decided it was time to start giving presentations in a different way, and in the way I felt most comfortable. I started preparing with a focus on the client and began considering what was important to them, such as: What information do they need? If I were in their shoes, what would I be worried about concerning this transaction? And because the two are different, did this client need to be educated or convinced?

After adopting this new approach, I went into a very important client presentation with the CEO, CFO, COO, and head of human resources for a Fortune 500 company. The objective was to explain the mechanics and strategy of how we were going to successfully execute a very large initial public offering and the techniques that we would use to maximize the price and the optimum distribution of the transaction. I had one colleague with me, and frankly his presence was a reinforcement to bring the real Carla to the table. I trusted him and knew that he believed in me to take this risk. In fact, he had used his professional and political capital to set up this meeting and have me involved. I had the undivided attention of the most senior individuals in the company and I brought the real Carla to the table.

The outcome was phenomenal. Rather than making a presentation *to* the client, I had a conversation *with* them. By the end of the meeting, they trusted who I was and that I would do a great job for them on the transaction. The next day the CFO made a point to call the most senior officer on the account to give *very* complimentary feedback and rave reviews about the meeting. It was not only a great accomplishment for me, but more important, I learned two of the most significant lessons to that point in my career. First, I learned that when you can turn a presentation into a conversation, you have won the battle of converting a client; and second, I learned that the real Carla was my best competitive weapon and my key personal advantage.

If I had brought my authentic self to those situations earlier in my career, I would have been able to focus on what was important: listening to the client, picking up on small cues of what was significant to them and responding quickly and creatively to their needs, and, no doubt, ultimately I would have created more productive meetings, a better professional reputation, and a steeper career trajectory for myself. I would have learned key lessons of my profession much sooner and could have been entrusted to take on greater responsibility earlier. I would have been able to build the trust that is the foundation of any client–banker relationship

because I would have communicated authenticity, not tentative-
ness, lack of confidence, or, worse, fear.

YOU WILL HAVE BAD DAYS

I have often asked myself, "Why or where did you lose your
voice? How did you suddenly become this quiet, insecure, unconfident person? What happened? Where did the real Carla go?"
I realized that the experience of working with a tough, insecure
person very early in my career had caused me to start to doubt
myself. The manner in which I received feedback from the person
was harsh and often made me doubt whether I had the capabilities
to do the job. If I asked them a question about an analysis I had
done, for example, they would sigh and say, "You don't do *that*!
What did you learn in business school? Go ask so-and-so down
the hall how to account for that specific tax treatment or how to
account for that in the model."

I knew that I had always done well quantitatively in school. In
fact, my college thesis was highly quantitative with statistics and
regression analysis. I had excelled in my finance classes at Harvard Business School, yet this person was making me question
whether I could do basic math and finance! Without realizing it,
my confidence had been busted and, as a result, I submerged my
voice. I was afraid to say anything for fear this person would challenge me and find something erroneous in my logic or analysis. I
didn't realize back then that the reason this person challenged me
every chance they had or sent me to their other colleagues to get
answers was that they did not know the answers! This person was
not a very good banker and was grossly insecure.

Insecure people are extremely difficult to work for because
they are preoccupied with being found out. They are always

afraid that someone will figure out that they are not as good as they seem to be or have advertised that they are. They go to great lengths to maintain their position, which includes trying to keep the people who work for them, especially smart people, on edge and at bay. When you are working for an insecure person and you do not fully own who you are, it is very easy to lose your authentic self because you are constantly focused on trying to figure out how to please them instead of being focused on how to improve your strengths and be your best self.

It is very easy to lose sight of your competitive edge, your authentic self, especially when you have had a few difficulties on the job, when your confidence has been busted, when you have a difficult boss, or when you think that your colleagues don't think very highly of you. When I heard that the senior woman I mentioned before didn't think much of my performance in meetings, and I realized that it was because I was quiet and did not participate in the meetings, I could have easily chosen to go further into hiding and clam up even more! I could have accepted that this was the person I had become and I would have to deal with it, which would have completely given away my power.

These kinds of things will happen to all of us periodically. However, what's important is how you choose to respond. You can become completely overwhelmed by the current challenges of the situation and not focus on the potential, triumphant outcomes that you ultimately want. You can begin to question yourself and your abilities. Worse, you can question your decision to be at the company in the first place, or question your potential success there. Or you can recognize this kind of thinking for what it is—negative, self-defeating thoughts, distractions that eventually will create a severe competitive disadvantage if you are not careful.

When you find yourself processing thoughts that focus on

what your colleagues think of you, how you can be more like someone else, why something will never work, or you become overly concerned with the potential pitfalls of a particularly strategy, know that you are submerging your best, authentic self, and are on the road to a disadvantageous competition where you won't likely be the winner. If you bring your fearful self to the table, the self that holds back on great, bold ideas, the self that is competitively disadvantaged, you probably will lose out on opportunities and ultimately not maximize your potential success.

We all have bad days. But when you find yourself entertaining these kinds of negative thoughts, stop dead in your tracks and refocus on these facts: You won this job because you were the best for the job. You are smart, quick to learn, and can quickly acquire any skill you might be lacking. Think of your strengths and spend the next week showcasing them in the workplace, while spending some time improving those things that you or others may have identified as deficiencies. Reorient the game so that you feel comfortable playing again—as you presumably did when you walked into that job—or decide, realistically, if it is time for a new seat, a new firm, or a new industry.

THE AUTHENTIC YOU AS A RELATIONSHIP BUILDER

When I talk about being all of who you are, I am not just talking specifically about work-related skills; I am also talking about bringing the other characteristics that you are proud of or that define you to the office as well. As I've already talked about, in order to build effective relationships, it is important that people get comfortable with you, that they feel they know who you are. This is the basis on which people decide whether they want, or can have, a relationship with other people. Relationships are an important key to your success in any corporate or professional environment. Particularly in transaction-oriented environments like investment banking, your ability to build effective relationships with your colleagues and clients will not only be the key to ascending in the organization; it also will have a direct bearing on your compensation.

One of the important things about bringing the other you to work is that those other characteristics might be the very things that allow you to establish a bridge toward building relationships with your colleagues and clients. Sharing your other self—your outside interests, such as your passion for mountain climbing, running, work with nonprofits, or sports—could very well be the ice breaker that starts that first conversation and eventually a relationship with a client or coworker. You never know who might have the same passions and interests as you, or who might want to learn something from you.

As you may know, I am a gospel singer. I have recorded several CDs and performed two concerts at Carnegie Hall. The spiritual part of my life is extremely important to me. I am an active member of a faith community and attend church regularly. I do not wear "holy roller" across the front of my business suit every day, but I am very comfortable alluding to spirituality or church in my casual conversations at work. You're probably wondering, "What does that have to do with success at work?"

Well, one day I was working with my team on pricing a deal, and it wasn't going well.

At noon I said, "Okay boys, it's twelve o'clock and I am heading over to St. Patrick's (the famous Catholic cathedral on Fifth Avenue in New York City, which is not far from my office) during lunchtime."

The guys immediately started ribbing me: "Oh boy, there she goes off to church to pray again."

Later, around four that afternoon, after we had priced the deal successfully, I said, "See guys, you made fun of me, but look at what happened. You know it was that prayer I said at church before." They all laughed at me and said, "Yeah, right! Whatever, Carla."

Did they make fun of me? Yes. But praying Carla is part of who I am. I did not feel uncomfortable with their ribbing, nor did I feel uncomfortable saying that I was headed over to the church to say one for the deal. My faith is at the center of my life; it is part of everything I do, including business. I could have let these guys make me feel odd or weird, but instead I stayed true to who I am and shared it with the people I work with. Do I need to hit them over the head with it? No. But I don't need to hide it either.

And you know what? Some of those same guys that like to rib me about praying? They are the same people, who, when something goes awry in their lives, will pass me in the hall, pull me into a conference room, and say, "Hey, Carla, I know you've got a hotline to the Man upstairs. I've got some trouble at home; can you send one up for me?" Being my authentic self has actually helped to create closer relationships between me and those guys than some of my other colleagues have been able to do. How about that?

Still not convinced? Consider another story about a woman who was on a panel with me a few years back. I'll call her Marissa. Marissa was a Latina, Spanish-speaking woman working for a big global consulting firm. As one of the first Latinas to be hired in her division, she did everything possible to fit in. She did not want to display any of the stereotypical behavior in dress or language that people often, no matter how mistakenly, associate with Latina woman. She even worked to get rid of any trace of her Spanish accent. When it came time for her company to give out a plum assignment in Latin America that she was well qualified for and had worked so hard to get, she was passed over for a young white man. He didn't even speak Spanish and was far less qualified for the position than Marissa was. Then why didn't she get the job? Because she had done such a good job at suppressing who she really was that those in charge didn't even see her as Latina. They didn't even know that she spoke Spanish! Even though it was widely known that a Spanish-speaking Latino would be the best person for the job, they never even considered her. Do you see the potentially disastrous results of not being who you are?

Here's another example. The year I got promoted to managing director, another division asked me to sing at their holiday party. Up to that point, I had tried to keep investment banker Carla and gospel singing Carla somewhat separate. When they approached me, my first thought was, "No way!" I didn't even work for this other division and I had no desire to give anyone in the company any ammunition to that could be used against me later. It was one thing to sing for my own department's holiday party, but for another division's? What would people think of me if I got up there and sang?

But then as I considered it a little longer, I began to have second thoughts. I heard that little voice inside, the one that with experience I've learned to listen to. I believe that voice is usually the Spirit trying to talk to me. It said, "Don't say no so quickly. I think you'd better go and sing that song, Carla."

So I told them yes; I agreed to sing at the party. As I was exiting the stage after my song, there was a guy waiting for me at the bottom of the stage steps. "Carla," he said, smiling at me and extending his hand, "I've heard so much about your voice. That was really terrific!" He introduced himself as a very senior person in that division. Since I was working in a different division, equity capital markets, we had never had any reason to interact. After I shared one of my personal passions and sang that song, we ended up having a long *business*-oriented discussion that gave him the opportunity to know me as a professional, as a banker. If I hadn't agreed to come to that party and sing, we may have never had the opportunity to meet. And guess who was the head of the promotion committee was that year? Because I was willing to let Carla the singer be present in an environment that was created because of Carla the banker, I had an opportunity to present Carla the banker to someone who needed to be exposed to me in that capacity. Days later when I was being discussed in the promotion committee, this person who recently had had a positive personal experience with me had a point of reference when he heard what was being said around the table about me. I feel strongly that being my authentic self *really* paid off that day!

SHARE ALL OF WHO YOU ARE

Most of us are not one-faceted, but rather multifaceted. If you stop to think about it, you are not just an investment banker, an editor, a lawyer, a marketing professional, or a salesperson. Most of us have outside interests that would qualify us to say that we are also artists, authors, skiers, or cartoonists. Whether you are a jock, a singer, a poet, or an antiques enthusiast, share it. Bring that person to work along with the professional you.

Talk about the things that make you unique, *especially* in jobs that are client centered. It is an easy and extremely important way to bond with and find common ground with your prospects and clients. Maybe your client likes Motown music, too, or is a math geek or a distance runner like you. Talking at work about my love for singing has served as an amazing icebreaker in so many of my relationships with my colleagues and, more important, with my clients. If they don't sing, then in most cases their kids do or they have a favorite artist, or at the very least they "have always admired people who can carry a tune." Your hobbies and interests could be exactly what open the door to a relationship that, over time, could help you seal the deal with a client, be invited to an important meeting, or be that added element that helps you get the promotion. If your outside interests are a large part of who you are, then use them in relationship building internally and externally. Thinking that your personal interests have no place in the workplace is a big mistake! They are an important part of who you are.

Consider the number of hours we spend at work each day. Most of us spend more time at work than we do anywhere else. It is not uncommon for Wall Street employees to put in up to twenty hours a day! To be at work that many hours and spend it trying to be someone other than who you are is a surefire way to unhappiness, eventual poor or compromised performance, and early burnout. If you are focusing on trying to be someone who you aren't, then you are using valuable intellectual capacity that could be used to learn and comprehend new product information, enhance your skills, or find out more about the political environment you work in and how to successfully navigate those choppy waters.

Even if you have to wear a "uniform" to work, it is important that you still bring all of you to work every day. Even in the uniform that I wear, I bring *all* of Carla Harris to the office *every day.* Has it cost me money or time, or both? It may have. Sometimes being your authentic self may cost you, too, particularly when the political environment at your company changes, such as when, for example, your division manager gets fired, your firm is acquired by another company, or your authentic self *really* clashes with someone who is currently in the power seat. In cases like these it will take you time to adjust and figure out how to be your best self and operate in the new environment. Just continue to focus on who you are and you will get back on track and find yourself successful in the long term.

One of the questions that I am often asked is, "How can I really be myself when the politics of my company dictate that I behave like someone else?" Or, "Just by virtue of playing politics, I am not being myself because I hate to be phony, and that's what it takes to play." I do not believe that you have to hide your authentic self in order to engage in corporate politics, nor should engaging in the politics make you become someone who you aren't.

Politics are everywhere, in every industry, in every department, and in every company. As I said in the beginning of this book, there are no true meritocracies, because people are involved in the evaluative process, in granting new assignments and promotions. Those people bring their subjective selves to the work environment, to their daily interactions, and to the evaluative table. Politics are formed where two or more people combine in an environment and a culture is formed. Politics follow because they define the rules in the culture. The trick of successfully navigating the political waters with your authentic self intact is to play the politics in a way that is comfortable for you.

I realized in year five of my career that it was important to bring my authentic self to work and that the *real* Carla was my competitive advantage. By the time I arrived at the coveted managing director's position, I was happy with the woman looking back at me in the mirror, even through the ups, downs, and disappointments. The triumph was that the authentic Carla had made it to the apex. The key for you, particularly when things get tough, is never to forget that someone else didn't get the job because *they* weren't the right person—you were. Things sometimes will get tough or difficult at work—that's inevitable in any job. But no matter what happens, don't submerge who you really are. Take the risk—bring the real you to work with you every day. I guarantee it is one of the best things you can do for your career, and it will make you successful in the long run in any environment.

CARLA'S PEARLS

- One of the keys to your long-term success in any organization is to own the person you *really* are. Bring the real you to work every day.

- Never forget—someone else didn't get the job that day because *you* were the best candidate with the most unique combination of skills and talent.

- In order to stay focused on remaining authentic and being the best original self you can be, you must first understand what your competitive strengths are and concentrate on improving your weaknesses.

- You personal life does have a place in the office—your interests and hobbies and the things that make you unique can be a bridge to building important relationships with clients and colleagues.

- Things sometimes will get tough or difficult at work; that's inevitable in any job. But no matter what happens, don't submerge who you really are. Take the risk—bring the real you to work with you every day. I guarantee it is one of the best things you can do for your career.

CHAPTER 2

BE THE ARCHITECT OF YOUR OWN AGENDA
Have a Flexible Strategy and Don't Be Distracted by Mistakes

In Chapter 1, I spent time talking about the importance of bringing your authentic self to work. One of the most important things that the real you can do is to construct your own career agenda. This is important because *you* are the one that has to live with the triumphs and the disappointments. *Only you* really know what matters to you in terms of time, money, and the pace at which your career progresses, and only you know what sacrifices and trade-offs you are prepared to make to achieve success. Part of being the architect of your own agenda is understanding what success means to *you*.

Too often we rigidly focus on a career plan that we think will take us to a desired position within a firm. Most of the time we are emulating the career plan of someone we admire, thinking that we can copy their plan and have the same results. We think that it will take us the same number of years to move from rank to rank. We think that we will have the same type of assignments and that we will work for the same set of executives as we progress.

In reality, however, we don't really know exactly how other people have arrived to where they are, what challenges they had to overcome, or what trade-offs, compromises, and sacrifices it took to get them there. Nor do we know why they chose their particular path and what they wish to accomplish in their career.

Observing what others do to achieve success is important, but it is equally important to design your own path, remaining cognizant of your industry's necessary skills and experience requirements and staying open to unforeseen developments and opportunities along the way—opportunities that could give you access to even greater career achievement or satisfaction than you could have ever imagined in your original plan.

This is one of the "pearls" I learned through a tough lesson. Early in my career, I was one of a few passed over for a promotion. I was angry, embarrassed, and upset, and, of course, I was ready to quit. In fact, there were several people telling me that I *should* quit, go to another firm, and essentially start over, because politically, at first glance, I appeared to be sunk! I also wasn't sure that I could continue to stay, try to do a great job, and position myself for a promotion the next year. I felt I had failed.

Thankfully, I had the sense to take some time to think. I went back to my original career agenda to review what I wanted to accomplish. In reading over my agenda, I was reminded that one of my goals was to be an officer of a major investment bank five years out of business school. I wanted to have the experience of working on complex, interesting, and high-profile transactions. I wanted to build my Rolodex of corporate contacts across various industries. Despite the fact that I had not been promoted that year, I could in fact stay another year, position myself for a promotion, and still achieve all of my goals without incurring the political start-up costs of moving to another firm and without the compensation risk of moving to a new environment without a guarantee. The reason that I was considering leaving was purely emotional, particularly since I was being assured by my boss that I had a great shot for a promotion the following year.

If I hadn't had my own career agenda and taken the time to properly analyze the pros and cons of leaving versus staying in the context of my ultimate goals, I would have been distracted with the disappointment of not getting promoted. I would not have focused on staying in an environment where I had some support, a track record of some previous wins, and a "chit," or IOU from the organization. To me all of these factors combined meant that there was a higher probability of achieving my goal at my current firm, instead of moving to a new firm where there would be so many unknowns. In the end, I made the right call. I was promoted the following year and stayed on track with my personal career agenda.

Here's another example of why developing your own agenda is so important. Gina was a vice president in a consumer products company. Her career agenda was to acquire marketing and sales skills that would allow her to rise through the organization to a position as the lead brand manager for a blockbuster product and to manage a team of people.

Midway through her sixth year in the organization, Gina was offered an opportunity to manage a small product that would represent the company's foray into a new area. She turned down the position because the product was new and appeared to have a fraction of the revenue potential, at least in the short term, of the blockbuster product that she was currently working on. Ultimately, it took Gina another six years to get promoted to lead manager of that bigger product, and by that time the product was considered a mature product and as such no longer the revenue producer it once was. In the meantime, the person who took on the new product grew it to a multihundred-million-dollar product and was promoted to the product's lead manager within three years.

Gina's mistake was failing to consider the new opportunity using her career agenda as the primary guide. If she had, she would have realized that the new opportunity would have exposed her to the skills and analysis that would have more quickly enhanced her marketing and sales capability, and in the end, because the product was new to the company, afforded her an opportunity to move up more quickly. The company was investing in making the product successful, and she would have been a net beneficiary as one of the first people assigned to the product.

Perhaps you are offered a job that's not the exact one you were hoping for. Before you turn it down, go back to your agenda and consider your overall goals. It could in fact be a good move. People who repeatedly find career success learn to broaden their perspective and understand that there are always several roads to getting where you want to go. Remember, the agenda defines the goals; the strategy of *how* you get there should always be flexible.

WHAT IS THE AGENDA? WHAT SHOULD IT LOOK LIKE?

Your agenda should contain both a macro perspective and a micro perspective. It should include your broad career goals, such as "I want to be in financial services as an investment banker," or "I would like to be in broadcast journalism and host a prime-time news show on a major network," as well as contain more specific goals, such as "I want to be in this particular department to learn about product X for two years and then move to a sales role selling the product," or "I want to do beat stories to get more comfortable with the camera before moving toward an inside anchor job." In addition, your agenda should include goals pertaining to compensation and promotions, as well as a timeline for attaining those goals.

When you are compiling the micro perspective section of your agenda, and, if possible, before you walk through the doors of a new company or start a new job, ask yourself these important questions: "Why did I choose to join this company? Is it for the compensation or the prestige? What do I want out of this job? What kinds of skills do I hope to learn? What experiences do I hope to have? What people do I want to be exposed to? What kind of time line am I on in terms of projects and promotion? How long do I want to stay with this company?"

By asking yourself these kinds of questions and thinking about your answers you are setting your own path; you are being the proactive architect of your own personal agenda. When you develop your own agenda, it will serve as your guiding motivation for your time at any organization and throughout your career. When times get a little bumpy or difficult at work—and they will at some point—you will be able to motivate yourself when your work or your boss is not motivating you if you have an agenda and can answer questions such as: "Why am I here," or "Why does this job, this assignment, this content make sense for me?" you will be able to get over the rough patch. You can use your agenda to remind yourself that you are pursuing *your* goals.

Your agenda will help keep you on track, help you stay in touch with your goals, and ensure that you garner satisfaction and enjoyment from your job on a daily basis. Unpleasant things will happen in the course of your career—that's reality. You'll get a bad boss, the market won't cooperate and you'll have some deals go bad, or there will be layoffs and management changes. By staying on your personal course you'll be able to stay focused on your goals and what you need to do, no matter what is happening around you.

I met Michele after a speech I gave at a conference. She worked for a company that was recently acquired by a larger firm. After the announcement there was a great deal of negative talk and gossiping among employees. Michele didn't believe in gossiping. Part of both her professional and personal agendas was that no matter what her position, she wanted to always be known as the person with the solution rather than the complaint. But as a result, she found herself beginning to feel isolated, not wanting to take part in conversations with her colleagues because they were always mean-spirited and negative. Michele wondered if she could manage her professional relationships at work without compromising her integrity.

Michele had done the right thing by not getting involved in the negative talk, because the new owners were paying attention for sure. It is my belief that corporate "chaos" like takeovers, mergers, and downsizing certainly can be challenging times, but rather than be viewed as negative, they should be seen as chances for opportunity. While everyone else is huddling in the hallways and ducking into conference rooms proselytizing about what's going to happen, spend your time looking for opportunities where you can excel. Stay focused on *your* agenda. Do not get distracted with change. Instead, consider how change can be integrated into your agenda.

That job you've been interested in? Look for opportunities to make a case for why you should have it. Start developing relationships with the new people coming in. There will be interviews to decide who they will keep and who will go. When you have the opportunity to go on your interview, be excited about the new company and the possibilities of being part of a new team. Take the opportunity to talk about the things you'd like to do, talk about the things you are good at, and where you see your skills fitting in at the new firm.

In terms of those negative-talking colleagues, I advised Michele to get herself back in the loop with them by inviting her coworkers out to lunch or offering to go on a coffee run for the group, but rather than participating in the negative talk, to keep her positive attitude. When negativity would come up, she should flip the conversation and talk about something positive. Sooner or later one of her colleagues will ask, "How can you keep such a great attitude?" This will be her opportunity to say, "This too will pass. It will all be fine." Soon her colleagues will start to get the idea and hopefully follow suit and begin to focus on solutions.

Or at the very least, they'll find someone else to complain to, knowing that Michele works to focus on the positive.

A personal career agenda will not only help you stay focused on your goals, but it will also help you develop strategies for how to achieve them. For instance, if you want to become a top executive in a corporation and you see that most of senior management has held overseas assignments or rotated through the marketing or finance department, then based on that knowledge you can chart your course. You can plan your assignments or choose to accept projects that you think will give you similar international exposure, financial skills, and marketing acumen to qualify for a senior-level manager position, rather than following the course of someone who stays within one area and tries to become more and more senior in that particular area over time.

If you are an associate in an investment bank, you know that in order to become an officer, you have to demonstrate that you can penetrate/influence client thought before you can become a vice president. You must be able to present your ideas to a CEO and in some cases to a board of directors. If you have not had presentation experience by your second year (see my example in Chapter 3), you know that you must seek it out, internally or externally through your work on community boards, in your church, or anywhere where you can learn.

Your agenda will help guide you to take the right professional steps. Without an agenda, it is easy to get distracted with what's going on around you or to get discouraged when you are having a challenging time in your career. Years will go by very quickly and you might find yourself stagnant in a no-growth position with no particular goals you want to accomplish. People often ask me, "How do you keep up the pace of an investment banker? After so many years, how do you still do it?" I can do it because I have an agenda. There still are things that I want to learn, deals that I want to make in tough market environments, and management teams that I want to meet. I am doing what I am doing and working where I am working because part of *my* agenda is to work with very smart people and to work on cutting-edge financial products in all types of market environments at a firm that is considered a leader in the space. I also want what I do to have an impact on a lot of people, and my professional agenda supports those goals.

IT'S NOT ABOUT KEEPING UP WITH THE JONESES

When you work in a team-oriented environment, or if you work for a large corporation and there are several other people on your team at the same level, it is often easy to become distracted with what is going on with other people. For example, suppose the associate in the cubicle next to you, who joined the firm at the same time, gets promoted before you. It is easy to become angry and jealous, and then to start to doubt yourself. The truth is, your not getting promoted may have nothing to do with you or your lack of skills; it could just be a lucky break for them. They could have been willing to make sacrifices that you were and are not willing to make or they could have had an aggressive sponsor who got it done for them ahead of time. You have to be careful not to overreact to these types of situations.

Curtis was promoted to senior vice president a year earlier than Hazel. They started at the firm at the same time and moved throughout the organization, receiving promotions simultaneously throughout their eleven-year careers. Technically they both would have been up for promotion a year from then. Hazel was surprised, upset, and ready to quit when she heard the news about Curtis. As she prepared to confront her boss, she thought about the previous year when both she and Curtis had been approached about working in Hong Kong for what was perceived as a tough two-year assignment. Hazel had been unwilling to go to a region where she thought the environment would be difficult to do business and to give up her lucrative domestic accounts. She also had been unwilling to uproot her family and give up her active life in San Francisco. Curtis decided to go to Hong Kong, uprooting his two children and interrupting his wife's career. Curtis's assignment was very successful, he returned to the domestic office twelve months sooner than expected, and was promoted early to senior vice president.

Consider the facts—Hazel and Curtis were offered the same opportunity, but Hazel had been unwilling to take the risk for that particular international assignment and to make personal sacrifices. Curtis had been willing to do some things for his career that Hazel had not been willing to do.

We each have our own likes, dislikes, preferences, interests, and personal lines that we will not cross. This is why we should not measure ourselves by others' report cards. Sure, it is important that you generally be in the rhythm of timing for promotions or new assignments, but they must be *relevant and right* for you. What is most important in the context of your career is that you are offered the same opportunities as everyone else, but that you recognize your choices may put you on a different timeline and compensation path than someone else. What matters is that your choices be consistent with your personal career agenda. Hong Kong did not work for Hazel for a number of personal reasons. As a result, she didn't get promoted when Curtis did. She realized that there was no reason for her to be upset, because she was still on track with what worked for *her* agenda.

If your goal is to get promoted, check where you are relative to your career plan. If you are relatively close, then return to focusing on your own agenda. If you are disappointed in the timing of your promotion, use your disappointment as a tool to engage with the key decision makers and do what's necessary to make the promotion happen. The goal is to create a "chit," or IOU, so that, assuming you continue to perform well, the organization feels like it owes you the next time.

Somebody is always going to be on top, and it won't always be you. Sometimes you have to be second, fifth, or seventh. If you think you always have to be number one, you are likely setting yourself up for major disappointment. One of the laws of the professional jungle is that every dog has their day. Everyone gets a shot at the top and at some point someone else gets their turn. There are politics, people, and other factors well out of your control that influence changes in organizations every day. The political winds in an organization can shift quickly—all of a sudden you can find that you have gone from having a lot of sponsors, mentors, and advisers to being completely unprotected in an organization, and therefore completely vulnerable.

Joseph had been waiting for an opportunity to play a leadership role in the newsroom. He had been a beat reporter, worked on special-interest stories, and taken on all of the tough, unpopular stories and assignments, in the hope of getting an opportunity to be the lead evening news anchor. Joseph wanted to be the person who directed the tenor of the news stories told by the station.

After two years of tough assignments, building internal relationships, and recruiting a sponsor who would help him to get this assignment, he finally forged a strong political relationship with Steve, the head of the station. Steve agreed to help Joseph with the assignments that would give him the prerequisite experiences to get the lead position he wanted and be respected by his peers and others in the newsroom.

Within six months Steve made changes in the newsroom that left the lead evening news anchor job open and available. Steve privately told Joseph that the job was his and had sent strong signals to the rest of the department suggesting the same.

A week before the announcement was to be made, Steve left his position as head of the station, citing major differences with the station's owners over the strategic direction of the station. The owners replaced him with the manager from a competitor station, and she brought over a colleague who she named to the lead news anchor position. Joseph decided to stay and continue to be a special-interest reporter, something he loved, and wait for another opportunity to move to the lead job.

Like Joseph, you won't always move or get promoted as fast as you'd like, and things won't always happen the way you want them to. That's where your agenda comes in. If your goal is to be promoted, then go back to your plan and make sure you are doing everything *you* need to do to reach your goal.

By allowing your agenda to guide your decisions, you take the emotion out of the process and create space to focus on what you want to achieve. There's no need to be upset that your neighbor got promoted before you, because your plan is in place for the same thing to happen to you. Having an agenda keeps you focused on yourself, rather than on what Howard or Russell is doing in the office next door. It also keeps you from making emotional, uninformed decisions like storming off and quitting the organization because one of your peers got promoted before you did. The truth of the matter is that moving to another organization might in fact put you on a longer track to your promotion. When you change companies you become the new boy or girl on the block, with no experience or political capital, and you'll have to prove yourself all over again. If rather than making a rash decision to quit and go to a new company because you are upset about something you instead choose to stop and focus on your agenda, you could properly evaluate whether or not that is the right decision for you. You may see that despite the setback, you can reach your goals faster in your current organization rather than move to a new company. You may still choose to leave, but choose to leave because it works for your agenda, not because you are upset or angry.

THE COMPARATIVE AGENDA WHEN MONEY IS INVOLVED

While I argue that you should be guided by your own agenda with regard to your assignments and pace of your promotions, I am not suggesting that you don't use the norms of what exist in your industry as a guideline. For example, if it takes three to four years to get to vice president and eight to twelve years to get to managing director, you use that information as a guide, not as law, for where you should be in your career and when.

The tricky part of the comparative agenda as opposed to your personal agenda is around the issue of money. While what other people earn shouldn't necessarily influence decisions you make about your own career, certainly some relative comparison regarding compensation is useful. You have to be cognizant of what's happening in the environment and in the marketplace around you. If you find, for example, an egregious inequality, such as your colleague making $100,000 while you are making $50,000 for the same job, that's a problem. I am not suggesting you settle for or tolerate an unfair situation. If you feel like you're not being valued or that your pay is out of whack and there is no reasonable explanation, approach your manager and ask why.

Getting compensation data is tough. Most companies will not want to give you comparative data because that information is confidential to each individual. However, you can ask for pay ranges at your salary grade level in order to assess where you stand in your class or rank. As you get more and more senior, the ranks or class are not as significant and you usually have to rely on out-side sources like your colleagues at other firms or headhunters for information. In most cases, headhunters are more than willing to give you the bands of industry pay levels for someone with your title. And it is always wise to use the industry data when talking to your manager about a pay disparity.

In any money- or pay-focused conversation you should be very direct and ask for what you think you deserve. You should also find out what is required to be in the top bracket of pay at your organization. These are not easy discussions to have, but it's your career, and if you are not prepared to have the conversation on your own behalf, then who will? This is an important part of your career agenda, in the same way that you have to manage the content of your job or your career trajectory. I believe in, "You don't ask, you don't get." I am not suggesting that you go and ask for more money all of the time. I am saying that if you think that you are doing a top-notch job and the organization acknowledges that, then there is no reason not to ask for top-notch pay.

Know what you want for yourself. Marginal differences such as your coworker getting promoted six to twelve months before you or getting four good assignments to your three are not worth focusing on and only distract you from your own career. If you perceive that someone else is getting slightly more money than you, again, if it is a marginal difference, it may not be worth using your political chits on that, when you may need them to bargain for something bigger down the road, something on your agenda that really matters to you.

Over the years, I've seen so many people get upset because so-and-so was making more money, or because someone else got a project they thought should be awarded to them. I've watched as they got all worked up to the point that they quit and went to work elsewhere. But the thing is, while it's possible the new company might be a better fit for them, what's more likely to happen is that they get to the new place and have to start all over, making contacts and connections, and establishing themselves at their new job. And as a result, it ends up taking them longer to get promoted than it would have if they had just stayed where they were. It's true that sometimes, when we're in the middle of it, the difference of a few months or a few dollars can feel like a colossal injustice. But even if it takes you six or twelve months, or even a few years longer than your colleague to reach your personal goals, you have to keep referring to your original agenda to remind yourself of your personal plans and the decisions and trade-offs that you are willing to make. Are you living *your* life the way you want to? Are you learning what you wanted to learn on this job? If the answers to these questions are yes, then what does it matter if you don't get promoted for a few more months when your career is likely to be years or decades long? The truth is your goals and aspirations are what matters most.

THE "THEY" SYNDROME

Part of the advantage of developing your own professional agenda is that you take responsibility for what is happening to you in your career. There certainly have been times when I have stopped along the way and compared myself to classmates who were advancing ahead of me or colleagues who seemed to be doing better then I was. It was a few years into my career when my confidence had been busted, I wasn't getting promoted fast enough, getting paid what I thought I should be paid, or getting the plum assignments that I wanted. Comparing myself to others, I started to question my abilities and wonder what went wrong.

At this point, I had not yet constructed my own professional agenda. And naturally, as we often tend to do, it was easy for me to look to blame my colleagues, the organization, or my boss for not treating me fairly. I call it the "they" syndrome. It's what you do when things don't go the way you hope and you find yourself saying, "They did this," or "They did that." "They won't give me a fair shot." "They just don't want to promote or pay me." When you find yourself saying "they, they, they" every time you start to explain why your career is not moving in the direction you'd like, then it's time to check yourself. Instead of blaming "they," which is a passive approach, ask, "What did *I* do to contribute to the situation?" To focus on "they" and what "they" did makes you the victim. When you live as a victim, you give away your power. To live in your power, you have to understand that you are participating in the situation in some way for it to happen in the first place.

I am not saying that "they" don't have some part in your career not going the way that you might like, but remember that *you* are responsible for your career success. Perhaps you have not been using the right politics with *them*, building the right relationships with *them*, asking of *them* what you want in your career. These are things that *you* are supposed to be doing.

When I found myself stuck blaming "them," I realized it was time to get honest with myself. I took some time to sit back and get reflective. I considered, "What happened here?" I realized that I wasn't necessarily doing all I could to move forward and that I was playing a part in some of my missteps. I hadn't exposed myself to the right people enough. I certainly had not initiated and developed the right relationships, and I certainly did not have enough supporting relationships in the firm. I didn't do my homework to find out how the organization worked. I thought projects had to be given to me. I didn't understand that I could go after projects and be proactive, and that I had the power to say no and turn projects down.

For example, there was one senior manager to whom I was assigned for many projects. I didn't really like working with her, as she was very difficult. But I was under the impression that because she requested me that she liked my work. It turned out that all of my other colleagues were turning her down because she was so hard to work with. She was extremely critical and made me feel stupid; in fact, working with her was very unpleasant to say the least. Once I realized I didn't have to work with her, that I could decide what projects I wanted to work on, I never did it again!

Figure out what you want. Do you want exposure? To collect a certain number of deals? To expand on a certain skill set? It's important to define what you want for yourself as opposed to what the organization or your manager's expectations are. Understanding who you are, strengths as well as weaknesses, outside of someone else's definition of you, is the key to setting and keeping on track with your own agenda. (On this topic, also see Chapter 1.)

In my career, anytime I considered going to a new firm, I went back to my personal agenda and asked myself whether I was on track for what I wanted to do. It may have taken me a few months or even years longer than some others, but in the end I was satisfied with my own progress. And the same will be true for you. If you aren't satisfied with where you are, then it's your job to figure out what you need to do about it, not blame the guy across the hall for getting what you hoped for.

Having an agenda helps you focus on your plan, what you want, and how you're going to get it. If you have your own agenda, you don't need validation from other people. It's certainly nice to be complimented and patted on the back. We all like to be motivated, but you cannot make it a prerequisite for your working hard or doing well in an environment. Unfortunately, you won't always get the "attaboy" or "attagirl" that you deserve; you need to put yourself in a position where you do not have to have it in order to stay motivated. You have to know what you are doing and why you are doing it, and know when you have done a great job. We spend so much time at work. You have to be sure you are there for *you*!

BE FLEXIBLE

By now it should be obvious that I am a big proponent of having a plan and strategy to execute it. Your agenda is a key tool for getting from where you are to where you want to go. Consider athletes such as Tiger Woods or Lance Armstrong. Their goals of winning the Masters Golf Tournament or the Tour de France weren't realized by simply wanting it to happen—they had an agenda, which included strategies around their training regiments that led them to their success. But in order for a strategy to be successful, you often have to be flexible enough to recognize when your plan needs to be changed or adjusted. I am sure getting cancer wasn't part of Lance Armstrong's strategy to win the Tour de France. But when that happened, he did what he had to do in terms of getting treatment, getting himself healthy, and then he returned to racing to win seven consecutive championships.

It's common to think that your career will take a straight path to wherever you want to go. But sometimes things will happen or you'll be offered opportunities that, at first glance, may look instead like you're getting off track or treading water. The path you'll take, the one that will get you to the senior executive spot or wherever you desire, may in fact be different from the plan you envision for yourself today. But later down the road, the choices you make eventually could allow you to skip four or five steps on your career path. Here's what I mean.

In my fourth year on Wall Street, I was working as an associate in the mergers and acquisitions (M&A) department when I learned of an opportunity to become the operations officer for the equity capital markets division. As operations officer, I would work directly with the head of capital markets and be involved in setting strategy, hiring and managing professionals, and setting budgets.

My first thought was, "Boy, I don't want to be off the line." Off the line means being away from a position with direct client contact and revenue-generating deal flow. But I thought it over and realized that the job would give me an opportunity to show what I could do in a new area. Further, it also would afford me more of a chance to express my ideas to a new group of senior executives, an opportunity I would not have had if I stayed in my current position. In addition to reporting to the head of capital markets, I would have exposure to other senior executives from across the investment bank as well, including the head of M&A, the head of equities, and so on.

You'll often have the chance to take assignments like this one that, at first glance, look like they are off the beaten path, not part of your agenda. While off-line-producing positions such as the head of recruiting, the head of diversity, or the head of process reorganization are not revenue-generating positions, they play extremely important roles in the company's overall strategy. Be flexible. Don't immediately say no to opportunities like these.

In fact, what you may find is that, given that exposure, you are able to move ahead faster than you would have if you had stayed on the line. The move to operations officer in capital markets really paid off well for me. I forged relationships with other business unit heads, which supported and accelerated my success in my product area. In addition, the executive running capital markets at the time I worked there eventually became the president of Morgan Stanley. Because I had worked so closely with him, years later when I had an issue, I went directly to him and obtained valuable career advice and access to other individuals who could help me to achieve my goals. Because I had accepted that off-line position as an operations officer, we had a relationship—he knew who I was, and he knew my work. More important, he was willing to act as a sponsor to me and help me to move to positions that I am sure that I would not have otherwise been considered for. (For more information on sponsors, mentors, and advisers see Chapter 5.)

If I had been inflexible in my plans and stayed an associate in the M&A division, I never would have had the exposure to him or the other professionals I met while working there, many of whom have assisted me in various ways throughout my career.

Here's another example. Hilary was a senior salesperson in a pharmaceutical company. Her agenda was pretty straightforward. She aspired to be the top salesperson with the biggest, most prestigious, highest revenue-generating accounts in the firm. And she was well on her way. Then the company approached her about starting a corporate marketing business to offer other benefits to existing accounts to differentiate the firm from its competition in the marketplace.

It wasn't in her plans, but Hilary took the job. She had to write a business plan, recruit employees, and do many other tasks she would not have been responsible for as a salesperson. The business became very successful. Following a management change, the new people in charge didn't view the business the same way and thought it was superfluous. At the same time, another pharmaceutical company was looking to get into this business. Not wanting to build the business from scratch, they purchased this unit. Hilary is now making two and half times what she was making before, and her career has been catapulted to a level beyond her wildest dreams.

Learn to be flexible enough that when your organization asks you to take a year in an administrative spot, an operations area, or some other area that doesn't seem directly related to your end goals, that you'll consider whether it could offer you some very important benefits and valuable experience for your career and fulfill some of the broader objectives on your personal agenda.

MANAGING MISTAKES

Keep in mind, there is no guarantee that if you are flexible with your career plan that you won't run into other issues. You've heard the old expression, "the best laid plans of mice and men" from the John Steinbeck novel? That applies to investment bankers, publishers, lawyers, or people in any profession. You can have a fantastic plan and still make a major mistake on the job that will make you feel like the world has come to an end.

If you have a seat in the organization, you earned it because you deserved it. The last time I looked, there were no corporations giving out jobs altruistically. If you make a mistake, even though you might feel like crawling in a hole, retreating is the worse thing you can do. It is human nature—we screw up and start to think, "I can't cut it. Maybe I shouldn't be here." But consider that companies spend so much time and money on people resources, recruiting, and training. I like to think they don't make many hiring mistakes.

The truth is that you have all the skills you need to be successful. If somebody wants to keep reminding you of what you did wrong, simply take them aside and say, "Listen, I learned from my error and now I am moving on." You need to let people know that if you do make a mistake it's an exception, not the rule. Maybe you need some support in your environment or could use more training, but you fundamentally have what it takes to succeed.

I once read a quote from Dr. Benjamin Mays, the great civil

rights advocate, minister, orator, and teacher to Dr. Martin Luther King Jr. He said, "Just because you stumble doesn't mean you have to fall." You already know you have what it takes to be highly successful in your company. Any mistake you might make is simply an opportunity to learn something about yourself, your craft, your business, your coworkers, your clients, or your firm.

You don't have to let a mistake transform into a distraction and pull you away from pursuing your agenda. A distraction occurs when you make a mistake such as ticking someone off, blowing a deal, not properly calculating a model, putting the wrong exhibit in a client book, sending a controversial memo, or some other goof-up. Then rather than focus on the truth, that despite this mess up you are still a smart, capable person with skills and personality to match, that you simply made an error, you start to beat yourself up and become paralyzed by the mistake. You constantly talk about the mistake to everyone who will listen, repeatedly apologize for it, and continue to highlight it, particularly in the eyes of others. Rather than learn from the mistake, you start telling yourself that you should have known better, that you should have seen it coming—shoulda, woulda, coulda! You get distracted.

Understand that mistakes are an inevitable part of learning, but the key to that learning is figuring out how to make the experiences you gain from the mistakes work for you. Do not let the fact that you made a mistake become your focus and a distraction; this only draws your energy away from moving forward in the direction of your goals. You must work to be forgiving of yourself and your mistakes. Seek to learn from them and quickly move on, and eventually, no matter what your career goals, you will achieve them with grace, professionalism, and much success.

The real truth is, simply by virtue of the fact that you were hired in the first place means you have what it takes to turn things around. When the mistake happens, and it will happen, make sure you don't spend too much time dwelling on it. Step back and understand the lesson and develop a strategy for recovery. This is a good time to reach out to your mentor or someone else in your network whose advice you value and trust for help (see Chapter 5).

Sherry was working on an emerging markets deal, and she didn't understand the process of allocating a transaction and the concept of a "naked short." She was afraid to ask any of her peers for help because she thought that they might think less of her for not understanding this important concept. It was not inconceivable that Sherry wouldn't have a grasp on this important concept, because she had taught herself most of the business. When she came to the department, no one had bothered to train her properly and she had to learn, observe, read, make mistakes, and figure it out on her own. The naked short concept had never come up before with other transactions she had worked on, so she had never learned it.

Sherry also did not want to ask her boss because she was certain that he was not one of her strongest supporters. She was afraid he would use the fact that Sherry didn't know this key concept against her during year-end evaluations.

So, instead of asking for help, Sherry guessed on the amount of stock to go short, and it was a big mistake. The next day, after pricing, the stock went up in the aftermarket and because Sherry had mistakenly decided on a large naked short, she had to go into the market to buy stock to cover it. This cost her firm some of the revenue it made from the transaction. It was a very *real* and costly mistake. It not only exposed Sherry's ignorance about the concept of naked short, but it cost the firm *real* money. Sherry was mortified and her boss made a kind of cause celeb out of the mistake. For weeks afterward, every time Sherry and her boss were in internal meetings, her boss found a way to bring up the incident and continued to reinforce the fact that Sherry had made a costly mistake. Sherry found it interesting that others in her department had made errors on deals, errors that had also cost money, but she had never heard mention of it after the first couple of days following the blunder. It seemed, however, that her error was being replayed over and over again for everyone to hear.

Finally, Sherry took her boss aside and said, "The mistake that I made was a huge one, I own it, and I learned that I will never go forward to make a judgment on my own when I *know* that I need help. I would like to think, and I hope, that you know when I make a mistake it's the exception and not the rule. I have *learned* the lesson from the error and it's time to move on. Do you agree? Do I have your support to keep moving ahead and to perform well, the way you expect me to and know that I can?"

Sherry's boss reinforced that she needed to rely on him for critical judgments if there was ever a risk of losing capital. He also took the opportunity to share some of the other skills that he felt she needed to improve. He closed his response by agreeing that she had the skills to do a stellar job in the department and that she should and could rely on him to help her. He also never brought up her blunder again in internal meetings.

Sherry's conversation with her boss was a pivotal one. First, it not only gave Sherry an opportunity to openly own the mistake, but it also allowed her to show her confidence by stating that she had learned something from it. Second, she signaled to her boss that she was aware of how he repeatedly acknowledged the mistake ("I have *learned* the lesson and it's time to move on. Don't you agree?"). She also communicated that she is conscientious, good at her work, and not typically prone to making errors. Third, she took the opportunity to engage him as a part of her success team by asking for his participation in the decision to move on ("Do you agree? Do I have your support to keep moving ahead to perform well, the way that you expect and know that I can?")

When you make a mistake, especially a costly mistake, own the mistake, acknowledge it, and declare to your boss and colleagues what you have learned, and then leave the experience. Take the blessing of the lesson and move on. Don't keep reliving it by constantly apologizing for the error and talking about it over and over again. When you focus on the mistake repeatedly, it can and will become a distraction because it takes your attention away from the fact that you are smart and qualified to do a stellar job in your endeavor. Stay focused on the fact that you have the intelligence, the skills, the experience, or the ability to learn quickly and excel.

One of the key components of your mistake recovery strategy is to just stop, learn, get rid of the emotion and the feeling of shame and burden, and move on. Don't allow the mistake to color your perspective about your abilities. When you make a mistake that is starting to distract you from the business at hand, remember a time when you did something really well, tackled a new project with ease, or handled a difficult situation. Go back and focus on the truth: that you have an excellent track record. Remind yourself what you did to be successful other times and how you moved forward. This is the truth that you need to rely on to get through this challenge: you have done it before; therefore, you can do it again.

LINE UP WITH THE CORPORATE ECOSYSTEM

Part of your micro or more specific agenda is to make sure you are properly lined up with what I call the corporate ecosystem. Along with your agenda, your success relies on being authentic, knowing who you are, and making sure that you are aligned with the right type of people in the organization.

There are two types of personalities in the workplace. One is the political maniac, and the other is the workhorse. The political maniacs are the ones with outstanding political skills; they understand how to attract, nurture, and work the right relationships in an organization for their gain. They are not necessarily the hardest working or the smartest people, but they know how to work the system to get what they want. The second type is the workhorse. The workhorses are the ones who follow the rules, work very hard, focus on acquiring key skills, apply them, and then ascend throughout the organization on merit of what they do rather than who they know. They work more hours than other people and are detail oriented, extremely smart, and reliable.

Each of us has qualities of both the political maniac and the workhorse, but the traits of one or the other is dominant in each of us. Once you identify which one you are, you can maximize your success, your pay, and your value by lining yourself up with that same kind of person in your line of authority.

For example, if you are a political maniac but your boss is a hard worker, you'll be valued for your connections and ability to make things happen, but you won't be rewarded. Similarly, if you are the hard worker and your boss is the political maniac, while everybody loves a workhorse—after all, they get things done— you will be valued, but you still won't be rewarded or compensated in the way you would like. Remember, being valued and being rewarded are two different things. You can easily be valued in an organization and not necessarily be paid well. People tend to value *and* reward traits that are similar to theirs—it is human nature. Looking back over my career, I can draw an exact correlation between times when I was lined up with that part of the ecosystem that is consistent with who I am as opposed to the times when I was not aligned and my level of satisfaction, or dissatisfaction, with my compensation.

The key to career success is to develop an agenda, a strategy to help you get from where you are to where you want to go, but with enough flexibility to allow you to be open to new opportunities. Use the test the waters questions that I discuss in Chapter 7 to recognize when your plans may need adjustment and when you might need to make a complete change. At some point all of us will make mistakes; it is a part of life. But when they happen, learn from them and move on—don't let them distract you from the end goals in your agenda and the chance to grow as a professional.

CARLA'S PEARLS

- Create your own agenda. Know who you are and what you want from your career, and don't spend a lot of time comparing yourself to others.

- Don't get caught up in the "they" syndrome. If you find yourself blaming others for your situation, step back, reflect, and honestly consider how you may have played a part in where you find yourself, then work to correct your errors.

- Be flexible. Don't be so attached to your plan that you miss opportunities to gain exposure or experience that could help you in the future.

- Don't let mistakes become distractions. We all make mistakes; it's part of life. Stop, learn from what you did, put your learnings in your professional toolbox, and move on.

- Line yourself up with the corporate ecosystem. If you are a workhorse, line yourself up with a workhorse boss; if you are a political maniac, line yourself up with a political manager. This way you'll be valued *and* compensated for your contributions.

CHAPTER 3

YOU ARE THE CAPTAIN OF YOUR CAREER
The Ninety-Day Rule

O ne of the biggest mistakes people make when entering a new job or assignment is that they think they have a long period of time to get up to speed. They think they can take their time getting settled before the organization expects valuable output from them. In fact, it is common for people to think that they have at least a year to learn their job and make a contribution to the organization. But in today's competitive environment, this is often not the case. In the fast-paced economy that we live in today and in the corporate environment of quick management change, no one should assume that they have at least a year to prove themselves. In fact, I contend that you have about one quarter, ninety short days, to create an impression of your value within any organization.

When you are interviewing for a job, when the organization is evaluating you, they are primarily assessing three things: your *can* do, your *will* do, and your *fit*. Your can do is your ability to do the job or their assessment of your future ability to do the job. Your will do is an assessment of your motivation, and whether or not you are likely to be a good team player, follow instructions, and get the job done. Both your can do and your will do are somewhat objective, with a thin overlay of subjectivity. Your résumé and your past experiences are what will substantiate both your can do and your will do. The most subjective judgment call that the organization is making about you and your projected success in the organization is your fit.

Your fit with an organization is indeed the most subjective and the most critical component to both your short-term and long-term success. The fit is assessed in answering questions such as: "Is it easy for you to get along with others? Do you catch on quickly to the formal and informal rules of the game? Do people seem to like you? How easily do you mesh within the organization or do you behave like a fish out of water?"

I have seen so many people not get past their early years at a company because of this subjective idea of fit. It is not tangible, it is not concrete, yet it can make or break you within an organization. Your first ninety days are critical in both laying the substantiating evidence, not only for your can do and will do, but most importantly for your fit.

In your first ninety days in any new job, assignment, or responsibility there are three things that you must accomplish to establish the foundation for what you can do, will do, and where you will fit into the organization: 1) you must learn the basic skill that is necessary to perform the job; 2) you must learn the unspoken rules of the game (the informal politics of the environment), and 3) you must get to know who the pertinent players are in the organization and understand the key relationships that you have to develop.

I find that keeping a detailed calendar is one of the best ways to stay on track. I am maniacal about time. I input everything I do into a time schedule in the hour, of the day, in the week, month, and year it will occur. I find that this is particularly effective for setting professional goals. It is very easy to get busy and distracted and not realize that three or six months have passed by and you are still behind with respect to establishing an important relationship, learning a new skill, or learning about a new product that is important in your business or some other goal that you wanted to accomplish.

LEARN THE BASICS OF THE JOB

In any job there is already a model of how it should be done. There is a certain way to build a merger model; there is a way to develop an ad campaign or write a consulting presentation. For example, in investment banking, with every presentation, each company has a certain way that it presents its arguments with respect to why it should win the business and a certain way it presents the company's credentials. There is usually a standard table of contents for every new business development pitch and a standard set of documents included in the presentation and processes followed for every deal execution or strategy implementation for each company. Every company and each industry has a standard way of doing things, and in your first ninety days, you should understand what the norm is before seeking to improve it. The first thing you must do is learn the basics and then set out to master them.

Ask yourself, "What are the key success factors of this project? How does this process or product fit into my company's revenue equation? Does it affect the cost side of the performance equation? What examples of this already exist? What is the best example? How do most people learn how to do this task?"

For example, if you are a new associate and you have never worked in investment banking before, the spotlight will be on your quantitative and analytical skills. You must prove very early on that you can build, understand, and analyze a model. You need to understand the basic principals of corporate finance and accounting, and you also need to know how to use and manipulate an Excel spreadsheet. If you have had no previous exposure to either, then you need to develop a plan, including a list of the people you will tag to teach you to learn the basics of modeling within a couple of weeks. You must then practice building those models on your own for the next two to four weeks. Hopefully you won't get an assignment for which you have to actually build a model before you have had a chance to familiarize yourself with some of the basic principals. If you do, then you will have to quickly accelerate your learning plan. Each financial services organization has its own way of calculating certain ratios or presenting certain data. Some investment banks even have a different way of presenting comparable company analysis, valuation comparisons, and even calculating weighted average cost of capital.

Timing is key here. Ninety days goes by very quickly and in a fast-paced, competitive environment, there is not a lot of time to make a second impression. If you are in a consulting environment, for example, in the first four weeks, you want to spend time learning the structure of different types of consulting studies, a merger integration presentation, a human resource related project, or a strategy study for a new product. Each study has its own format for presenting data and drawing conclusions. If you are working in marketing, you'll need to know the company's target markets, what products your firm sells, the key selling points of each product, and the competitive environment. The key is in your first ninety days to find out what the key metrics are for your company and for your particular job and learn them.

SEEK OUT TRAINING WHEREVER YOU CAN

Notice, I have not said that it is imperative that you have someone train you. The unspoken rule of almost any organization is that you must take the initiative to figure out those things that you do not know and need to learn. Most companies offer basic training modules. For example, investment banks present a four- to six-week training course for analysts and associates designed to give them the basics in accounting, finance, capital markets, and modeling. While these training modules are good for introductory purposes, you really learn what you need to be effective and successful once you start the actual job. These training courses give you a good foundation of what you will need to know, but you are responsible for finding the information, reviewing presentations, and practicing modeling on your own.

Furthermore, you cannot rely on the more senior team members you work with to teach you what you need to know. While technically it may be their responsibility to train you, they may or may not be able to do it. You may be assigned to someone who is very good at what they do, but they may not be a good teacher, or you may be assigned to someone who has been lucky in their career to do okay but has never fully mastered some of the basic concepts and, therefore, cannot really teach you. In both of these cases, you must take the initiative and get the information on your own.

If you reach the six-month mark in your job and find you are deficient in a key skill, you will not be able to rely on the excuse that "no one taught me." The organization won't likely question or penalize itself for not properly managing or teaching you. Instead, it will have concerns about your ability to take initiative because you did not aggressively seek out the knowledge you needed.

Most companies love to tout their wonderful training departments, and in many cases the training programs are good and effective, but don't *expect* that the organization is going to push you to get the training you need, nor should you wait to be trained. If organized training modules are offered, take advantage of them.

Plan to be aggressive about making sure that you learn the basics of what you need to know to be effective. If there is a training module on effective financial modeling and you are an investment banker, take the course. If you are going into sales and trading, and derivative products are something you'll need knowledge of to sell, take the training module as early as possible in your career. If you are in a support position, such as an executive assistant or a sales assistant, and your company offers courses irrespective of rank or department, take them! You either will be able to leverage these courses internally as you move upward and throughout the organization or you will be able to use them to position yourself for something better in your next job. While most major organizations have extensive development resources, it is your responsibility to take advantage of them and get any training, formal or informal, that you need. Remember, you are responsible for the day-to-day management of your career (see also Chapter 2).

Yes, an organization will provide people, tools, seminars, classes, and experiences to help you develop skills and be successful, but no one is going to closely monitor you to see if you have a skill deficit or urge you to quickly correct it. Organizations are more apt to assess your skill set during evaluation periods, and then it is too late, because in a performance review you don't want to hear that you have a skill deficit that impeded you from getting a promotion or that caused you to miss the top echelon of pay. If you are offered training, schedule the training and make it a priority to attend. If you aren't offered training and you think you need some, seek it out.

The truth is, people won't always have or wish to take the time to make the investment in your development. If you are in an assignment-oriented job, for example, who you are teamed up with is a significant factor in determining how much you will learn. If you are working with a very smart, well-respected person who is an ace at their job, then you'll probably learn a great deal. But if the person you're working with isn't so great, and this is likely to happen at some point in your career, you may have trouble getting the information and training that you need. These types of people are often likely to be very insecure. Often they are afraid that their deficiencies will be exposed. Insecure people are very difficult to work for and nearly impossible to learn from.

In either case, you can't just sit and wait for someone to come along and offer to help you. Ninety days is a very short period of time, relatively speaking, but in corporate terms it's a long time to waste without learning something. And at the end of that quarter period, you are going to be expected to know the key elements of your job. So if you're not getting trained where you are, you'll have to look for other opportunities internally or outside of the firm on your own time, making sure you have the skills and information you'll need to do your job.

As a banker, one of the most important abilities I wanted to acquire was to learn outstanding presentation skills. I had hoped to develop these skills very early in my career, but because I did not attach a time frame to my goal, I found myself two years into my career without the relevant experience that would make me an outstanding presenter and speaker. I knew it was an essential goal to accomplish before becoming a vice president in the next two years. I needed to be able to express myself effectively and confidently in front of a corporate board of directors.

Finally I realized I had to get serious. So I applied the ninety-day rule. I wasn't getting chances to present much in the course of my job, so I gave myself ninety days to seek out occasions to work with strong presenters whenever I could. I actively sought out internal opportunities, such as volunteering to make recruiting presentations on various college campuses. Then I gave myself another ninety days to seek out opportunities outside of work to practice being a persuasive presenter in case there were no chances at work to do so. I volunteered for a number of nonprofits and because I worked on Wall Street, I would always get approached about serving on the finance or the treasury committees. Over the next three to six months, I took on leadership roles there so I'd have a chance to practice presenting numbers in a compelling way, just as I eventually would have to do for any number of corporate boards when presenting a deal for my day job. I did it as often as I could and practiced as much as possible, so when the time came, I would be ready.

As a result, as I approached my promotion to vice president, I found that I had mastered the art of making effective presentations and it was no longer a potential impediment to moving ahead. If I had not been strategic and methodical about acquiring those skills, with the volume and the intensity of work that I was responsible for on a daily basis it would have been easy to make excuses and let my goal fall to the wayside, allowing it to become a barrier to moving ahead in the organization.

If you find that you cannot find avenues to the training you need outside of the firm either, I will argue that this is still no excuse. In that case you have no choice but to teach yourself. Read, go to the library, search the Internet, do whatever you have to do to learn what you need to know to help you master the basic skills of your new job or assignment in the first ninety days. There will be a time when you will be tested, and you'd better be ready if you want the impression about you to be a good one.

This is not to say you have to become an expert in that first quarter. But you really must concentrate on finding some way to make an impact, to "put points on the board," so to speak, in that first ninety days. You must demonstrate that you have a familiarity with the basics necessary to function in your new position.

You want to show that you are a smart, quick learner and that you know the critical elements that will allow you to be successful in that position.

This is an important point, because it's the first ninety days you are in a job that dictates your success trajectory. It is usually around this time that the company starts to assess if it has made a good hire. If you make a good impression and the opinion of you is good, the trajectory will lean toward outstanding. People will think you are a smart, capable person with great potential to add value to the firm. You have succeeded in starting to establish your "halo." You have heard of the "halo" effect: Once people think you are smart or that you are really outstanding in your job, then essentially you can do no wrong. Going forward, people's view of your work and your ideas generally is positive all of the time. People listen to your ideas expecting to hear something positive, something value added. They assume that your work or your conclusions are right until they learn otherwise, and generally no one goes out of their way to prove you wrong. In the event that you make a mistake, you are given the benefit of the doubt.

On the other hand, if, after three months, you have made a mistake or the projects you've worked on have not gone very well, and there is a question about you or your work, or if someone has made a snap, false, or unfair judgment about your abilities, then the trajectory of your career will point toward average or, worse, needs improvement, and that's not good. If you get that label early on, each assignment you do get becomes an exercise in proving yourself. You are not likely to be chosen for the meaty, challenging, or high-profile projects that ultimately could develop you to be outstanding in your position. Most jobs are really designed for on-the-job training, where you essentially learn by doing. If you don't get an opportunity to do, you don't learn effectively. When you are considered average or in need of improvement, you are on track to get stuck in the middle of the pack with the other mediocre performers, and you will have a tough time even getting an opportunity to really show what you can do.

The way to avoid the curse of mediocrity is to keep a record of what you are accomplishing along the way and advertise it. In Chapter 2, we talked about establishing an agenda for what you want to accomplish, the skills that you must acquire, the type of experiences that you must have, and the relationships you want to build. As you are accomplishing the items on your list, keep a record, and along the way articulate to your manager, team, and boss the experience that you now have under your belt. By day ninety-one, start talking about what you've done, about what you've accomplished, and the points that you have put on the board. Proactively reach out to your manager and other people you work with and let them know about what you've done, the things that you have learned, the deals or projects that you have worked on. Talk about what you liked and what you didn't like about your assignment. Talk about the lessons you learned and what you are interested in pursuing in the next three to six months.

You want to plant the seed that you're not only a smart, capable team member, but that you are focused on getting up to speed quickly and progressing in the organization as soon as is practicable. That is the perception that you want to create as the new person on the block. Don't wait until you have been in the job for six months or, worse, at your annual review to start wondering about what impression others in the organization have about you—by then it's too late to easily create or change an impression or perception. Don't give people a chance to form an impression, especially an incorrect one, completely on their own. On your first day get started creating and managing a positive impression of yourself, your abilities, and your work.

LEARN THE UNSPOKEN RULES OF THE GAME

There is a culture within every body of people, at the company level, at the division level, at the departmental level, even at the floor or the group level. If you want to optimize your opportunity for success very early, then within the first ninety days in that environment, you want to identify and adopt either the spoken, but more important, the unspoken rules of your environment, or rules of the game.

The rules of the game are commonly identified as the politics of an organization. These rules or politics cover everything, including how people communicate with each other, what buzz words they use, how people dress, and how and when they go to lunch. It also includes things such as how and when you approach the boss for a promotion, if or when you should expose other team members' mistakes (or does everyone participate in taking one for the team?), and what meetings are important and what meetings can be blown off. The rules will cover which social functions are important to attend and participate in. Is there an annual department football pool? Is there a certain way to approach senior people in the group? Are junior people expected to really speak their minds or are they generally expected to agree with senior people's ideas?

For example, on most teams there is a certain language that people use when they are countering someone's point in the group. In other words, the rules will tell you whether you should introduce an opposing idea by saying, "That's a terrific idea and here is something that I would like to add," or whether you should say, "I have a completely different idea that I think can add more value." The rules will let you know if you can challenge others by saying, "This is why that idea does not hold water," or whether you should say, "That's an interesting idea, but let me pressure-test the idea with this thought." All of these different examples are ways of saying the same thing, but depending on the political rules, one way of saying it will be more effective than another.

Another example of a spoken rule of the game is the departmental meeting. Let's say you work for an investment bank and there is a departmental meeting every morning to discuss what has happened overnight in international markets. The spoken rule is that the meeting is every morning at 7:30 a.m. No one ever says that the meeting is *mandatory* for you to attend, yet everyone in your department is on deck every morning at 7:30 a.m. for the meeting. That is the unspoken rule.

Consider this illustration of an unspoken rule regarding attire on casual Fridays. Now everyone has a slightly different idea of what casual attire really means. However, if you look at most corporate environments, there is an unspoken code. In an investment banking environment, the unspoken rule for casual attire generally means a name-brand polo shirt or a tailored, starched button-down shirt with no tie, a pair of khaki pants, and if there is a client meeting, it may include a navy blazer. In a technology environment, casual is much more relaxed and could mean jeans and fatigue pants with a casual top. No one will tell you specifically how to dress, but it is expected that you will adopt the informal uniform code. If you don't comply, generally no one will say anything to you, but you might find that you are not being included in important meetings with senior people or with clients, and that could be the reason why.

There are informal rules regarding lunch, midafternoon coffee, and after-work drinks, and you should adopt these rules quickly. We all know that during the workday lunch is important! If the group goes out to lunch every day, then you should go. I am not saying that you have to do it every day, but more often than not, you want to comply with the rule. This is one of the quasi-social rules that will help you to build and strengthen your internal relationships very early on. If your group is like a trading floor environment where most people eat at their desks, then you want to make sure that you go to get lunch at the same time that everyone else is heading down and to bring it back to your desk to eat it, particularly in the first ninety days. If the group goes to a certain restaurant or bar every Thursday, make sure to go, invited or not. Use these opportunities away from work to build your relationships. If there is a ringleader who decides where the group is ordering food from every day, make sure that you get an opportunity to do your part on behalf of the group. Is there a 3 p.m. coffee run every day? Who goes to get it? Does it rotate?

Understanding some of the informal rules, the unspoken rules of the game, will help you to become a part of the fabric of the organization very quickly. In the first ninety days it can be an easy way of establishing key relationships that will become the foundation for your success going forward. And if you are considered to be part of the fabric early in your career, you increase the probability that you will acquire and maintain that halo effect that we discussed before. If you can identify what the rules are and start to play within those rules every day, you can hasten your adoption into the group. You create a perception that you will fit right in. You put yourself in a position where people want to help you, because you are perceived to be one of the gang.

When I first started in the financial services business, I was in mergers and acquisitions and it was clear that M&A professionals had a culture of staying late and sometimes all night to get projects done. I am typically an early riser and would prefer coming in at 5 or 6 a.m. and leaving at 9 p.m. instead of coming in at 8:30 or 9 a.m. and leaving at midnight or 2 a.m. While I could have done what was easiest or most familiar to me, I would have missed an opportunity to build a rapport with my colleagues and have the chance to create relationships that were useful to me while I was in the department. By keeping hours I was more comfortable with, I would have been able to complete my work, but I would not have been considered a part of the broader team, a part of the fabric of the department.

It was the same thing when I transitioned to capital markets. In capital markets, professionals tend to come in early and stay until 7 or 8 p.m. No one ever told me that I had to get in by 7 or 7:30 a.m., but I was quick to see that if I did not get in at that time, I was foregoing a valuable opportunity to speak with my colleagues about what happened in overnight trading or what was said in the *Wall Street Journal* that morning. I would have missed the chance to build rapport away from the deals that we were working on. You must remember that you cannot go it alone in any corporate environment; you have to be considered as part of the team, and the first ninety days is the key time to make that happen.

When I am doing public speeches on the pearls and I talk about fitting in, being part of the gang, I often get the question, "What if they don't include me?" or "What do I do if everyone else in the group goes out every Thursday or Friday night after work for drinks and they don't invite me?" My answer: Invite yourself! If you see everyone else getting together in the department to hang out for an hour or two after work, don't wait to be invited—just tag along. No one is going to uninvite you, and if they do, then you have something you may have to report to your boss or someone else in the department. It may also be the case that you *assume* that people are getting invited to the weekly event, but it may be that no one gets invited; it is just a habit that has been formed over the course of time and everyone just knows to come along; and there you are waiting to be invited and are therefore excluded.

In other cases, you could be working in a very rough-and-tumble, up-or-out environment, like sales and trading, public relations, advertising, or even publishing, where people want to see what the new kid is made of. They want to assess whether you are rough and tough enough to fit into the environment, and there may be some informal hazing going on, where they don't invite the new people along to see how they respond. You don't want to fail the test by remaining on the outside waiting for the "you're in" sign. You can demonstrate that you are ready for the environment by taking the risk to be included, to step to the plate and go along with everyone. Don't wait for a sign from someone that you are part of the group; just behave like you are and that you're happy to be there from the beginning. You must remember that you got the job like everyone else, you intend to succeed in the organization like everyone else, and you intend to be a team player like everyone else, so act like it.

Does the group socialize together outside of work? When? How often? Social settings are the easiest way to start to assimilate into the group and can help you build important relationships, particularly in your first ninety days of work. As people get to know who you are, they start to feel more comfortable with you and are more apt to help you and are more comfortable forming mutually beneficial relationships with you. In my own experience, I have found that women, particularly women of color, are much more guarded about who they are and what they want to reveal about themselves. There is an unconscious and sometimes conscious attitude of, "there is my work self and my at home self, and the two don't mix." As a result, they are not apt to reveal those parts of who they are that could be important relationship bridges for them with their colleagues.

If you tend to have a skeptical nature, or are still uncomfortable about bringing all of you to work, then before you start the project or the job, decide what part of who you are you feel comfortable about revealing and trade on that until you are more comfortable with revealing more and tapping into the power that is demonstrated in being comfortable in your own skin. If you are bringing your authentic self to work, as I discussed in Chapter 1, then it will be much easier, early on, for you to feel comfortable revealing more of who you are and starting to create that important comfort zone between you and your colleagues and between you and your bosses, relationships that you will be able to leverage for your success.

Some of the excuses that I often hear from people regarding mixing socially include: "I don't drink, and all they want to do is go out drinking every week—how can I go out and do that?" or "I work in a very male-oriented department and all they talk about is sports, and I don't know anything about sports, and as a result I am never included in the conversations. I don't have anything in common with them!" In your first ninety days, you *must* find a common bridge of things to talk about if you are going to fit into the fabric of the group and the organization. I was not a big sports enthusiast before I joined the M&A department, but I noticed every Monday morning during football season, my colleagues would be discussing the weekend's games, key players, and who was ahead in the football pool. Since I wanted to be integrated into the fabric quickly, I called my father (who is a *big* sports enthusiast) every Sunday night to get the lowdown on all of the games and the names of four or five key players. I would walk in on Monday morning and say things like: "Did you see that Giants game? What about the quarterback for New Orleans—can you believe he was sacked three times; did you see that last play?" I took control of what could have been an uncomfortable situation for me and initiated the conversation. These questions invariably would get the conversation started in the office, and I was included! I didn't sit around all weekend and watch the games, but I learned just enough to be dangerous! I was included in the conversation, and I did not feel like I was compromising myself or not being authentic. My goal was to be a part of the conversations in the first ninety days, and I used my family network to help me. It was part of further substantiating my fit with my colleagues.

Can you imagine where I would have been had I gone for ninety days and not been a part of the daily informal conversations with my colleagues? When senior people observe your performance and are assessing your fit, they are also observing how you interact with other people at your level, and that informs and influences their perception of who you are.

In going out socially, particularly to events where there might have been a lot of drinking, if I didn't want to drink, I didn't drink. I would order a club soda with a lime. That drink looks like a gin and tonic! I didn't have to compromise myself, nor did I make my colleagues who may have been enjoying a cocktail or two feel uncomfortable because I wasn't drinking. I could laugh and talk and have a good time like everyone else.

It is a good habit to find ways of making the social interactions comfortable, particularly if you are in a client service business. You will often have to go out to social events, dinners, after-conference outings, sports events, and the like with clients. If you have been successful in using social events with colleagues to build your relationships, you will find that you can transfer those skills in building client relationships. In a fast-paced environment like investment banking, you don't have a long period of time to build a relationship with a client. Sure, that relationship can be strengthened, fertilized, and further developed over time, but it is in the first one or two meetings with a new client that they are going to decided if they want to build a relationship with you and if they can trust you over time. Remember that the more comfortable people feel with you, the easier it is for them to trust you. If people feel that you are being your authentic self, then they naturally start to feel that they can trust you, because you are courageous enough to be who you are.

Other unspoken rules of the game include how people are assigned projects, when they are considered for promotions, and positioning yourself for top pay. There is a how-to to all of these unspoken rules in any organization, and in the first ninety days you should not only observe how things happen but ask questions of your mentor or your adviser (see also Chapter 5).

Don't think that you can effectively differentiate yourself by not following the informal and formal rules of the game. Not while you are trying to move up the ladder. Instead, use your intellect and your work as your differentiating factor and use your demonstrated understanding of the rules as support for establishing your fit platform. Most of the time, the rules regarding projects and opportunities are not clearly advertised, but, particularly in your first *thirty* days, if you observe, you will quickly see how things work and how you must position yourself to take advantage of the rules. Understanding how assignments or opportunities are given will be key to navigating to the right trajectory, especially early in your career.

For example, in many investment banking departments, both product areas and industry verticals, there is an assignments associate. This person is responsible for assigning all of the new analysts and associates to various projects. As the senior people win business and determine the size and the composition of the team they will need to complete the assignment, they turn to the assignments associate to get junior, associate, and analyst resources allocated to work on the deal. Technically, the assignments associate is supposed to evaluate the needs of the deal team and match the skill capabilities and the developmental needs of the associate when choosing an associate for the assignment. In reality, however, more often than not, associates are assigned because they are specifically requested by a more senior team member or they happen to be an associate with time capacity at the time of the request. This is the unspoken process within the organization.

In reality the system may work for you if the assignment associate chooses you because you have time capacity and the deal happens to expose you to a type of assignment or product that you have not been exposed to before but need in order to round out your skill set. But consider if you did not know how the system really worked and you are waiting for someone to carefully evaluate your skill needs and match you up with the appropriate deal to give you that exposure. Practically, you could be waiting a long time for this to transpire, or it may never happen! Sometimes the pace of the business does not allow for this type of careful matching, and if you don't recognize this unspoken process, you could find yourself with an experience or skill deficit if you don't know to actively go and request certain types of deals or exposure from the assignments associate.

Another unspoken rule is that any associate can actively request certain types of transactions. They also can request to work with certain senior people or they can approach senior people outright and request to work with them. This informal rule is not advertised anywhere; you have to observe or be told by someone that it is okay to do this. If you didn't know this rule, you could also find yourself in a disadvantageous position, taking on whatever assignments are given to you. But by taking this passive approach, you never attempt to guide your assignments toward those things that will give you broad exposure to people within the organization or to products and experiences that you can leverage for other assignments going forward. And that's a mistake that will likely hurt you in the long term.

LEARNING THE KEY RELATIONSHIPS

Another part of the unspoken rules of the game involves the relationships that you need to develop and nurture. We have already talked about the importance of establishing the peer relationships in your first ninety days, but you also need to establish a few key senior relationships as well. You need these relationships to learn the how in how you get things done in your first ninety days. In most cases, you need these relationships to get the right assignments and the right developmental opportunities early on and, in fact, throughout your career. Remember that your work product alone will not lead to success in an organization—you need key relationships in order have your work positioned and viewed in the most positive light.

Ask yourself who the go-to person is in this department or division. Who is the key decision maker? Who is the person or persons who will decide when and if I can move to the next rung in my career? Which person is an expert in my product or process? Who is the person that is the facilitator in the organization? The answers to these key questions will point you in the direction of the people that you will first need to develop relationships with as you start your new job or assignment. These are the people who can teach you the things that you need to know or point you to the people who can. These are also the people who should be made aware of your progress, your enthusiasm for the job, and your desire to move toward greater responsibility. Clearly there are other relationships that will be important to your job and, more important, your career, and I will talk about them more in later chapters, but the people that can fit the above questions are the ones you will need to start to building relationships with in your first ninety days.

POST THE FIRST NINETY DAYS

After you have mastered the basics of your job in the first ninety days, you want to start to show what many companies refer to as significant value add, or put points on the board, as I like to call it. You want to show the organization that not only are you a quick study with good analytical, quantitative, marketing, selling, organizational, and client development skills, you also want to start to show what those skills can do for the organization. You want to foreshadow that continued investments in you will yield good returns.

For example, if you are in a sales position, after the first ninety days, you want to demonstrate willingness to approach new clients or further penetrate an existing client. If you are in a consulting job, you want to take a stab at pulling together a pitch or a study on your own. If you are an investment banking associate or if you are a new lateral hire, you want to show that you can build strong relationships with clients and have someone on the client side comment about you.

Also after the first ninety days, you want to start to hone the skills that you have been working on in that first quarter. Remember, I said that you did not have to be an expert in the first ninety days, but in the next ninety days, you want to start working on knowing your craft so well that you are on your way to becoming the go-to person for that product or process. You want to earn a reputation first among your peers and then with people senior to you as someone who knows the product/process inside and out, someone who is accessible and who is looking for ways to build upon the knowledge and make it better for the team and the firm. The aim is to set yourself up for feedback in your formal evaluation that says you learn quickly, you apply your knowledge and skill set effectively; you are an outstanding team player, always willing to help out and always looking for a way to take things to the next level. Typically you will receive feedback and/or a performance review a maximum of twice per year in your first zero to two years on the job. Most companies will at least give you some kind of informal review at the six-month mark, particularly in the first year. There is a lot that can happen to your career in those 180 days between your six-month and annual reviews. You can miss important assignments or miss exposure to products that might make you more effective with your clients, for example.

If your organization does not have these important checkpoints before your formal review, then you want to be proactive about asking for feedback. Choose three or four people that you have had consistent interaction with and obtain their summary view of your performance. You do not want to wait until the one-year mark to hear formal or informal feedback, because if the message from the organization is that you are behind, it's already too late. You are behind the eight ball with respect to catching up with the rest of your peers.

To stay on top of your game, closely monitor your peers, those who are just a couple of steps ahead of you in seniority and who are doing well. Assess their knowledge and seek to acquire the same understanding. Your organization may also have skill requirements for certain levels of seniority, as mine does. Look on your company intranet site, or ask your manager or HR department for a copy. Review the requirements, and make sure you know what they are so you can easily see what is expected of you at each level, and deliver those expectations at a minimum. The real goal is to deliver performance and a work product that "greatly exceeds expectations." If you feel you still need clarification, this is a good time to seek out the advice of your mentor. (For more on mentors, see Chapter 5.) Ask them what the company considers to be a star performer at your level. What characteristics do they possess? What skill sets have they mastered? You must know what's expected of you in order to successfully fulfill the requirements of your position.

I cannot tell you how many women, particularly women of color, I have encountered at various levels within different types of organizations who do not have a clear, concrete idea of what it takes to progress through their respective organizations. I was also guilty of this at one point in my career, particularly in the later years, as evaluations tended to become more and more subjective. If you cannot answer for yourself clearly what it takes to advance to the next level, then you should directly ask your manager, the decision maker, what the requirements are in their mind for you to advance. This action gives you two advantages: One, it communicates directly that it is your intention, your aspiration, your goal to advance, and two, it yields you a direct answer from someone who will be a decision maker in your advancement, which should give you a concrete map of how to move forward. You create an informal understanding with that person that if you do what is required, as they have defined it, then you will obtain your desired result.

At six months, your boss, human resources, and countless others are going to take a critical look at you and your performance to date. So at the end of ninety days, do a self-evaluation and figure out which skills you're missing and which you need to work on or acquire. Don't hesitate to solicit informal feedback from your boss at the ninety-day mark to pressure test your own perception of how you are doing, even if you believe that you are doing very well. Make the conversation very positive, with the objective of gaining greater insight into how to improve your ability to add value. Your discussion might go something like this:

I wanted to spend a few minutes to discuss my progress to date. I feel like I came and jumped right in full speed ahead and have quickly attained proficiency in _____, _____, and _____. I have really enjoyed working with _____, and _____ and have learned a tremendous amount from my client exposure in the last two transactions (interactions). As I look forward to the next quarter, my plan is to focus on _____, _____, and _____, but I wanted to check in with you to see if there are other things that you think I should add or change.

While this discussion is somewhat specific to one I might have in financial services, you can certainly tailor it for your industry.

One note of caution: Never simply ask, "How am I doing?" You do not want to appear insecure about your performance in any way (unless things have not gone well and you and your supervisor knows it). If things are going well, though, lead with a positive, confident discussion. This way you communicate that you are cognizant of your performance and that you want to make sure that the organization is as well.

If things have not gone well in the first ninety days, your conversation might go something like this:

I wanted to touch base with you to get your perspective on how things have gone this first quarter out of the gate. I feel like I have gotten the hang of things and have mastered _____, _____, and _____, despite a rocky or slow start. My learning curve was a lot more steep than I had originally anticipated and there were a few more things that I had to master to get to this point, but I feel like I have acquired some very valuable lessons in this first quarter and I am well positioned to leverage these lessons into solid value-added output. I am very interested in hearing your perspective to date and how you think I should most efficiently and effectively move forward.

This dialogue acknowledges that you have made mistakes, but that you have worked hard to correct them, you have embraced the data, the skill, the knowledge, and now you can leverage that to move ahead. You are also communicating, albeit subtly, that you do not intend to follow this bumpy road again and that you are looking onward and upward. You are not dwelling on the mistakes; you do not view them as irreparable, nor should the organization view them that way, and you are seeking guidance on how best to move ahead. All are positive messages, which is what you want to communicate. You never want to dwell on your mistakes, particularly mistakes that you make in the first ninety days. If you dwell on them, they become albatrosses, they eat away at your confidence, and they create a competitive disadvantage for you.

You also want to create an environment in which your boss feels comfortable offering you honest feedback. If they sense that the discussion will be difficult, they are less likely to give you the honest feedback that you really need at the outset of your new career, job, or assignment. This feedback is necessary for you to successfully progress, so do not create a situation where you stifle the flow of this critical information.

Following your ninety-day feedback discussion, you'll have the next three months to get up to speed and be ready to walk into your six-month evaluation and state with confidence, "I have the necessary skill set to succeed in this job and I am looking forward to more responsibility." The next big evaluation of your career will be made after one year. You want to arrive at the one-year evaluation on par or ahead of your peers from a skill and experience perspective. If you are already behind at this point, it will take a long time to catch up.

CARLA'S PEARLS

- It is very easy to get busy and distracted when we start a job, but make sure you take the time to write down your goals and schedule the time frames within which you want to complete them.

- Ask your manager, supervisor, or HR rep, or go to the company Web site to find out what is expected of you at your level and the level that you aspire to. Start to perform the functions of the level that you aspire to six to twelve months ahead of when you desire to get the position.

- Give yourself ninety days to master the basics of your job.

- On day ninety-one or thereabout, seek to have a meeting with your manager to informally discuss your progress and find out what things you need to work on prior to your six-month evaluation.

- Seek out training internally and externally, and, if necessary, seek to teach yourself.

CHAPTER 4

PERCEPTION IS THE COPILOT
TO REALITY
How People Perceive You Will Directly Impact How They Deal with You

One of the most important lessons I have learned during my career is that *perception is the copilot to reality: How people perceive you will directly impact how they deal with you.* The reality of who you really are or who you think you are can be largely irrelevant if others have the wrong perception of you, because people will treat you in a way that is consistent with who they *think* you are. The truth is, most of us would be very surprised to learn that other people's idea of who we are is often *very* different from how we *think* of ourselves. How people perceive us directly affects how they deal with us and how they treat us; we therefore have to make sure their perception of us is what we want and need it to be.

This is a little understood reality of achieving success in business: **You cannot assume that if you work hard people will notice you and think of you in a positive way.** In a true meritocratic environment, all of the evaluative measures are objective and everyone is equally given opportunities based solely on their abilities. But since the reality in any organization is that there is a subjective portion of the evaluative equation for success, perceptions as well as facts will sway the conclusions. In other words, what people *think* of you will influence the outcome of your performance evaluation, the assignments you receive, the clients that you are assigned, and, ultimately, your level of pay and your promotions.

For example, if you are perceived as quiet, nonconfrontational, and someone who "always goes with the flow," you are less likely to be perceived as a leader and the more aggressive personalities within the organization are more likely to try to take advantage of your seeming meekness than they would someone who they perceive would not let them get away with their aggressive behavior. Alternatively, if people see you as a no-nonsense professional who takes no flack, they are more apt to imagine you in a leadership framework. Therefore they will be more likely to approach you with the facts, respect your opinion, and be less likely to try to pull one over on you because they believe you will call them out.

If people think you are smart or politically savvy, they are likely to approach you differently than they would approach someone they think is not so intelligent or who is naïve about the environment. It is critically important for there to be a positive and powerful perception of you in the marketplace. The marketplace includes the work environment, the social environment, and any other environment where you are trying to accomplish your goals and succeed.

The question to ask is: "What do people think of when they say or hear my name?" If you are in a financial services organization, do they think that you are analytical, quantitative, and a strong relationship builder? If you work for a consulting firm, do they think that you think fast on your feet, that you are solution oriented, or that you pick up concepts quickly? If you are an engineer, do they think that you are a linear thinker, a great problem solver? If you are a teacher, do they think that you are a master at implementing the latest teaching methodologies, at engaging students, at producing great educational outcomes in your classroom? If you are a lawyer, do they think that you are a creative problem solver, that you are an expert negotiator, and that you have an excellent command of the law?

I can't stress enough how much learning this lesson about

perception has impacted my career; it helped me tremendously in advancing to a senior level. Just as companies create a marketing plan to influence how consumers think to encourage them to purchase certain products, you are creating a perception about yourself to encourage people to respect your judgment, to buy your ideas, and to buy *you* as a product.

You want people to see the professional that you want them to see, the stellar professional that you think you are. You also want people to properly evaluate or consider who you are as an individual. You don't want them to look at you and see you through the lens of their previous experiences with the person previously in your seat or someone who looks like you.

HOW IS A PERCEPTION ABOUT YOU CREATED?

+ Your Self-Presentation
+ The Baggage of the Beholder
_____

The Perception about *you* in the Marketplace

The perception that exists about you in the marketplace will be a function of two things. First, there is your self-presentation, or what you are putting out in the market about yourself. Second, add to that the impression people have about who you are based on the experiences *they* have had with people with similar characteristics or who look like you—what I call the baggage of the beholder, or what they bring from previous experiences.

It is important that you are cognizant of your behavior, speech, and dress, particularly in the workplace, because it is the foundation of the perception about who you are. These are the things that you present to the marketplace about you. You must actively think about the perception that you want to create and make sure that what you do, what you say, and what you wear are consistent with that behavior. If you want to be taken seriously in the organization, then you need to make sure that all three components are consistent with the environment, as I discussed in Chapter 1. If you want to be considered for an officer level promotion, you cannot dress like a junior person, for example.

I knew of a young lady at a financial services firm who was up for promotion. She was an outstanding associate but wanted to be promoted to vice president. As an associate, you are highly valued if you are resourceful, a real go-getter, have strong quantitative and analytical skills, and can build presentations effectively. It was clear that her bosses considered her to be a highly effective associate. However, most associates tend to dress a little more casually than more senior people and many associates don't spend what most senior people spend on wardrobe. Of course, that is because there usually is a discernable difference in the compensation levels between associates and more senior personnel. This woman told me that she wanted to be considered for promotion, but the senior people in her area seemed to continue to treat and address her more as an associate than as an officer. She was not asked to present first in meetings, her opinion was rarely solicited, particularly if more senior people were in the room, and when she was asked to talk it was to give the background assumptions and not the meat of the presentation.

My advice to her was to make two small changes: change her dress to be consistent with other women officers in her area and prior to group meetings discuss with her direct boss what she was going to present. "Have a premeeting, before the meeting, to discuss the strategy of presentation—that's what most officers do," I said. I told her to "suggest" to the senior person how the meeting should run, and what part she wanted to play in the process of the meeting. As a result, her direct boss, who was very senior, started to *perceive* that she wanted to and *could* play an officer role. In fact, he became more and more comfortable with her conducting the meetings. Because she looked (dressed) and spoke like an officer, they started to treat her like one, and she subsequently was promoted as she had desired.

I know that you're thinking: "That's not all there is to it! You can't dress your way into success!" No, you can't. This person clearly had the skills necessary to move to the next level. She had proven herself by the objective measures, but it was the *subjective* things that easily could have delayed her promotion by a year. If her boss had not perceived that she was ready, she never would have received the promotion. Part of the perception is created by what people *physically* see and what exists in their mind's eye. In order for you to be successful in moving up in an organization, the powers that be have to *perceive* that you are ready or worthy, or physically see that you are already behaving upward toward the next level in rank or pay.

In addition to your appearance, your behavior and speech also impact how people perceive you. For example, if you are always soliciting other people's opinions before you make a decision, then rather than being thought of as a consensus builder it might be perceived that you are incapable of making a decision on your own. If you are always commenting about why things won't work instead of finding solutions, then people are likely to see you as someone without good business development skills or who is not commercial, because rather than seeing a way to get to yes, you only appear to see no. If you are always belittling other people in meetings as a way to make yourself look more important, then the perception of you will be that you are a bully and cannot build consensus. Further, people probably will think you'd have difficulty leading or motivating a diverse group of bright new business professionals. On the other hand, if you are generous with the "attaboys" or "attagirls" for the people on your team, particularly if you are in a position of authority, and you are known for using words such as *we* and *us* rather than *I* or *me*, then you'll be seen as a great leader for whom people would want to work. How you behave, what you say, and how you say it, is the foundation of the perception you establish about yourself.

THE BAGGAGE OF THE BEHOLDER

The perspectives that we all hold are a function of the experiences we have had. That is a reality for all of us. Our experiences color our subsequent perceptions, which is human nature. For example, let's assume that you had a doctor who was very detailed oriented. She was a great doctor, but she had a gruff bedside manner. You know that she completed her undergraduate degree at Yale and graduated at the top of her class from Harvard Medical School. She did her internship at Mount Sinai hospital in New York City and has been in practice for twenty years. Still, you had a tough experience with this doctor because her people skills left something to be desired.

Let's assume that the next doctor you went to got her undergraduate degree from Yale, also graduated at the top of the class from Harvard Medical School, and also did an internship at Mount Sinai in New York City and has been in practice for twenty years. Now, if this person says something even slightly stern or direct to you, you probably are going to jump to the conclusion that she, too, has a poor bedside manner. Or once you learn that this doctor has the same credentials and profile as the first one, you are likely to evaluate her even more closely and focus on her poor people skills and bedside manner even more. Further, you are likely to have a negative impression of those skills because of your previous experiences.

People are prone to make gross generalizations. Most people think that the majority of bankers are type-A personalities, tough to deal with, and even ruthless. Most people assume that lawyers are cocky and arrogant. People think that Ivy League students are pompous and pretentious. It is these gross misperceptions that are either informed by an interaction that someone previously had or formed because of a perception that was created by observing the person from afar, or based on poor third-party information. It is therefore easy to understand why someone might approach you with a bias, especially if you do not look like them. Sometimes that perception may be informed and sometimes it may not be. The important thing to understand and accept is that we all do it and realize that it is something to work through like any other potential work challenge. You cannot control what experiences other people have, nor can you control how they affect them, but if the person is open-minded and fair, then whatever perception they may have about someone who looks like you can be positively affected by their interaction with you.

I am often asked, "How do you deal with knowing someone has a certain perception about who you are and your capabilities because you are a woman or, particularly, because you are a woman of color?"

The first thing I do is to remind myself that if they are meeting me for the first time, then they don't know anything about me firsthand; I did not contribute to any perception they already have. Second, I tell myself to be careful *not* to pick up their baggage and carry it as my burden. Carrying someone else's baggage will weigh you down and create a competitive disadvantage that does not exist for others in the workplace. Third, I look at it as an opportunity to educate. I say to myself, "I don't know why this person has an issue with women or black people, but I am going to make this such an extraordinarily positive experience that it will positively affect the next person they deal with who looks like me." I do not consider this to be a burden in the least, but rather an opportunity to make an even greater impact than just executing my job well.

It is important to understand *how* perceptions are formed and informed. If you can dissect how and why people think of you the way they do in the workplace, then it is clear what you need to do to further substantiate or support a positive perception. Or it will reveal what you need to do to change a perception that doesn't help you move toward your goal of success. Of the two components of the equation—self-presentation and the baggage of the beholder—it is infinitely easier to change a perception by adjusting the self-presentation component.

HOW DO YOU KNOW WHAT PERCEPTION EXISTS ABOUT YOU?

Before you can change a perception that exists about you in the marketplace, you have to know what that perception is. If you are not sure what people in your work environment think about you, then you should endeavor to find out. You cannot change or fix what you don't know. How do you find out what the organization thinks of you? You solicit the feedback formally and informally. In some cases, you can learn what people think of you through informal feedback from your colleagues. For example, suppose your coworkers make comments such as, "You are so detail oriented," "We can always count on you to give us the straight truth," or "You should bring up this point in the meeting; Bob really respects your opinion." You can deduce from these types of statements, particularly if you are receiving this informal feedback from more than one person, that the organization *perceives* you as an organized, straight-talking, honest, no-nonsense professional whose opinion is respected. When there is a clear and powerful perception of you in the marketplace, you will tend to hear these types of comments regularly. When you start to hear consistent comments from varied sources, then you know that your perception is a powerful and pervasive one.

Alternatively, if people are saying that you are "harsh, a tough critic, a challenge to work for," you could deduce that people may not think of you as a leader, a motivator, a team player, or someone great to work for. This type of perception in the workplace might, in fact, prohibit your superiors from choosing you as a team leader or someone to head a department. After all, you cannot lead if others won't follow.

You can also find out how the organization perceives you from the formal feedback that you receive in your performance evaluations where your strengths, weaknesses, and accomplishments are discussed. Since most organizations only give formal feedback once a year, it's not a good idea for you to wait until then to discern the perceptions that exist about you. By the time you have this annual discussion you will have lost valuable time—those twelve months could have been used to change a harmful perception. In the twelve months in between formal annual reviews, work to solicit informal feedback or test the feedback that you get from more formal channels.

Choose four to six people and ask them for feedback. First choose two or three people who do not appear to be your biggest fans. Then choose two or three people who you know are clear fans and ask for their perspective of your strengths and suggestions for things you should work on to make you more successful in your current role. The purpose of asking these questions is that you'll not only get a very clear picture of what you need to work on to improve your skill set, but *you will also have the chance to build more effective coalitions in the organization*. You need to be open to the possibility that the nonfans may have legitimate reasons to have a poor perception of you. If their perceptions of you result from a competitive perspective, and even if they have personal biases against you, just knowing this will help you deploy your energies to try to change their perceptions.

For example, suppose you did something directly to or in front of a nonfan to create a negative perception toward you. By meeting with them you'll have the chance to either explain or justify your actions or create an opportunity to work with them again and counter that experience in the future. If they are insecure about you, you can focus on reinforcing that you are a team player and that you are working to add value to the team, not just to promote your own cause.

It may not be easy to solicit credible or useful information from your nonfans. But like any other challenge in business or in life, this is an opportunity to learn. If there is someone you interact with on a regular basis who doesn't seem to like you, call a meeting. I generally recommend that you have these types of meetings in an environment where it is easy to have a conversation, like breakfast or lunch at a local café or at a coffee house rather than sitting down in an office with a desk between you. Sit down at the table like equals and have a conversation. It could very well be that you are mistaken, that they like you just fine. It is more likely that their perception of you is simply wrong.

A mistake we often make—and this is especially true of women, particularly women of color—is that when we get the feeling someone doesn't like us, we run as fast as we can in the other direction. Men certainly do this, too, but as women we often want to avoid conflict of any kind. And to avoid it, we are going stay as far away from anyone we think doesn't care for us.

But I say that that's the wrong approach. By sitting down with a nonfan and presenting your concerns, you are starting a dialogue.

You are on your way to positively affecting the perception they have about you. Ask for their advice by saying, for example, "I'd love to get some feedback on how you think I presented myself in the meeting today." Or try "How do you think I interpreted the numbers at last week's client meeting? Do you feel I articulated myself well?"

This is an especially important tactic if you are working in a smaller organization, where perceptions are formed quickly and spread easily from one person to another. If someone has formed a negative opinion of you and they are vocal or powerful in the organization, that person's perception can quickly become the perception of many. Unlike in a larger firm where you may be able to avoid dealing with certain people, in a smaller organization, avoiding that person who may not like you is not going to serve you well. The misperceptions could become "noise" in the environment, and you can't have noise in your relationships with people at work. It not only impedes your success in moving up the ladder; it's also draining and sets a negative tone for the office.

Approaching your nonfans can be a little intimidating at first, and you may not feel that you are getting very far in the initial meetings. The way they approach you may not change immediately; it may take two or three such meetings to change their minds about you and your abilities. But in all likelihood, they eventually will see the value you bring to the company and be recruited to your success team.

In the case of the people who are *not* fans of yours, you will create a different impression of who you are in their minds simply because you solicited their opinion. You send a very clear message that you are interested in their opinion, and that you also intend to try to be the best professional that you can be. You also create a platform for you to return to them for feedback at some point in the future. You can use this feedback loop to establish a better relationship with them and, hopefully, either recruit them to your success team or have them as a valuable part of your network.

It is important that you understand the negative perceptions that exist about you so that you can work to change them. As you become more and more senior or seek to move upward within an organization, the subjective information that exists in the marketplace will be a larger determinant of how and if you move upward toward greater and greater responsibility, authority, and power. Hearing positive feedback certainly makes us feel good and is always helpful, but it's the noise that exists in the marketplace, usually fueled by negative *perceptions,* that can impede your progress.

As you seek to get the formal and informal feedback, you may find an inconsistency in the feedback you get from junior people or colleagues versus that which you get from more senior people or your boss. When this happens, examine whether there is a difference in the person you are showing to your boss and the person you are showing to everyone else. If there is a difference, ask yourself why. Is it that you are going overboard to please your boss and ignoring everyone else? Is it that you are more comfortable being your authentic self and bringing your best self to your colleagues and not as comfortable or confident with your boss? Why? The ultimate goal is to have everyone in the organization have the *same* positive view of you. As you seek to bring these perceptions into alignment, you should start by first creating the positive perception with your superiors and your direct boss.

First, your boss's perception is often the hardest to change because you may or may not have daily in-depth interactions with him or her. Without frequent contact, every encounter has to be high impact and more effective in setting and reinforcing a perception. If your interactions with your boss are spread out over long periods, then it will take even longer to change or create a perception. This is why it is important to work to affect your boss's perception first. Last, the boss is often the most influential person in the environment and their perception of you can be subtly, informally (sometimes formally), and unconsciously passed down within and throughout the organization. Your boss's perception of you and the way they convey that perception to others will be quickly seen and interpreted by your colleagues and peers; another reason to seek to impact your boss's perception first.

CREATING THE PERCEPTION YOU WANT OTHERS TO HAVE

In an ideal world, you will focus on what you want the organization to think about you before you walk in the door. In most cases, we do not do this, because we are preoccupied with the fact that we have a new job. We want to fit in as quickly as possible and we want to learn what we have to do to be effective, when we should be focusing on creating and managing a perception. We generally start to focus on the perception issue when we get that first formal feedback, our annual review, or even later in our career. No matter when you start to focus on creating and managing a perception, there is a way of creating that perception and conditioning people to think of you in the way you want them to.

You must be able to describe yourself in a way that will make people remember you the way you'd like. The easiest way to do that is to ask yourself this key question: *"How do I want people to describe me when I am not in the room?"* Then identify at least three adjectives you would want people to use when they talk about you when you are not present. Why is this important? Because all of the major decisions about your career are made when you are not in the room and can't speak for yourself! Decisions about your compensation will be made when you are not in the room. Decisions about your promotions will be made when you are not in the room, as will decisions about new assignments. Decisions that will affect your career will be made *when you are not in the room.*

In any business environment, other people are constantly speaking about you, deliberating about you, or speaking on your behalf to clients, to each other, or to your superiors. When they speak about you, you want them not only to be complimentary and fair; you want them to highlight the qualities and strengths that you think are important. You want them to have a thought in mind about the person you are when they're making decisions that affect you, and you want to make sure that the thoughts they have are the right ones.

WHO, ME? NOT TOUGH?

I learned this lesson the hard way. I had been in investment banking for five or six years. I was working hard and assumed that because of my hard work that I was well perceived by everyone in the company. After all, why wouldn't I be? I was doing everything *I thought* I was supposed to do. Then one day during a conversation with a very senior managing director, he said, "You know, Carla, you're obviously very smart, and you're clearly a hard worker, but I don't know if you're tough enough for this business."

I was shocked! I thought that I had differentiated myself because I was a diligent hard worker who kept her head down and who knew the necessary information for her to do her job very well. I didn't understand that those things didn't give me any kind of competitive advantage and on their own wouldn't enable me to succeed.

"Okay," I thought to myself, "you can call Carla Harris a lot of things, but not tough? Are you kidding me?" My initial reaction was to wonder if his comment was *real* feedback, or if he was just yanking my chain. I decided that I couldn't take the risk either way. Rather than get upset and angry at his misperception of me, I asked myself, "What if he is *not* just giving me a hard time? What if he is not the only one who thinks this way about me? What am I doing that would make this guy, or other people here, think that I'm not tough enough?" Believe me, on Wall Street, the last thing you want to be thought of, particularly if you are a woman, is not tough.

Wall Street is a rough environment and very important decisions are made quickly, often with tremendous amounts of money at stake. You cannot be afraid to take risks, you often have to render judgments on incomplete information, and you have to be decisive when doing so. You cannot seem timid or appear to waver. Consider capital markets, where I worked. Clients depended on me and my organization to execute capital raises or render advice that it is critical to their company's ongoing competitiveness and success. If a client perceives that I cannot make good, sound market judgments, particularly in tough market environments, then I am not likely to be awarded their business or be a part of their transaction team the next time around.

I decided if that managing director's perception of me was really that I was not tough, then I was going to change it. For three months, I was going to walk, talk, eat, and drink tough! Anytime I spoke I would try to use the word *tough* somewhere in the sentence. If someone approached me and asked me to look over their analysis, I would say, "You better make sure it's right, because you know I'm tough!" If they asked me to sit down with their management team and critique their road show presentation, I would say, "Are you sure you want me to sit down with them? I don't want to hurt anyone's feelings, because you know I'm really tough!"

I kept doing that over and over, every chance I got. Three months later, I happened to be walking down the hall behind a team that was coming to see me and I overheard the vice president of the group saying, "Oh my gosh! I hope this is right! Did you do this? Did you do that? Did you double-check the assumptions, because you know Carla Harris, she's so tough." He was sweating!

It is important that you understand this point because I believe it is one of the primary reasons I was able to advance in my career, even turn it around at a critical juncture when it wasn't going the way I wanted. I recognized that despite my impression of the job I was doing, the smart, no nonsense, go-getter that I thought I was somehow was *not* present in the environment or was not *perceived* to be present. I could have ignored his comment and chalked it up to his personal bias, but I strongly believe that had I done so, eventually I would have become an irrelevant player in the organization. By changing the existing perception and presenting myself as a tough, no-nonsense decision maker, someone who stood her ground, unafraid to make decisions, I gained more respect from junior people, my peers, and people who were senior to me.

People always say to me, "I can't change anybody's perception of me; I am who I am." If you think that, you're wrong! You *can* change how people think of you simply by changing the way you behave, the things that you say, and the words you use when you are speaking to them. You can train them how to think about you by the way you repeatedly describe yourself when you are around them and by **consistently** exhibiting behavior that is congruent with what you want them to think of you.

TEACH PEOPLE HOW TO PERCEIVE YOU

Let's go back to those three adjectives again. When thinking about three words you would choose to describe yourself, keep in mind that those adjectives must be ones that are consistent with who you really are *and* be attributes that are valued within your organization. Whenever I discuss this topic before a live audience, inevitably the following question comes up: "How can I be authentic and be what the company wants me to be at the same time? It seems impossible."

I cannot stress enough how vital it is that when you are choosing the adjectives to describe yourself that you base them on who you *really* are. To understand who you really are will require some work on your part, especially at the outset of your career, when the choices and decisions you make can set the stage for your future success. You must invest the time and effort to sit down and do some thinking, carefully considering who you are and who you want to be.

Get out a piece of paper and write down your strengths and your weakness. What do you like to do? What don't you like to do? What kind of environment do you want to work in? What skills do you need to work on or improve?

Once you have the answers to these questions, *then* you can consider what the company values and what it wants to be, determining where the two intersect. Like we talked about in Chapter 1, you have to be who you really are in any situation to find lasting success. Imagine spending twelve to fourteen hours a day at work—an average workday for many workers in corporate America—and the whole time trying to be something you're not. It would be absolutely exhausting. Believe me, it's a perfect recipe for burnout! If you choose adjectives that aren't really you, it's conceivable that you may have some short-term successes, but that strategy won't work well for you over the long term. You will not be able to create and sustain a perception that is consistent throughout the organization. Further, imagine that you are successful in convincing people that you are someone that you are not. Then, as a result, you will have to go through life pretending or trying to be someone else. Why would you want to do that?

Once you determine your descriptive adjectives, the key is to establish a perception of yourself or to change a misperception, if one exists (such as what I did with walking, talking, and eating tough), you must then behave consistently to support and emphasize those descriptors.

In choosing adjectives that are valued by the organization, consider the key attributes for success in your industry. For example, let's say, like me, you work in investment banking. The organization will value descriptions like possessing strong quantitative, organizational, and analytical skills; relationship builder, team player, and time-management expert; and client-focused. Suppose you are in consulting; that means you'll want to consider choosing adjectives such as solution-oriented, linear thinker, logical, and flexible. If you are in marketing or brand management, you'll want to use words such as: creative, organized, possessing strong sales and market analytical skills, and critical thinker to describe yourself.

In short, you have to make sure that the adjectives you use to paint a picture about yourself are consistent with what matters to the organization. Why? Because then you will matter to the organization. Another key to choosing your adjectives is to consider your company's business model. Then look to find adjectives that are consistent with the model. Ask yourself questions like, "How does my company make money? What skills does the organization value? Who am I as far as this company is concerned? How do I describe myself? How do my colleagues describe me? Why am I important to this company? What critical role do I play? Am I relevant?"

Think about what the recruiters told you the company was looking for when they hired you. Look at your firm's annual report, read through its marketing literature, and in today's e-focused world, go to the company Web site. All companies put their real selves, or at least who they want people to perceive them to be, as well as what they value, in their marketing material. Find adjectives to describe yourself that will align you with the way the company values itself. Figure out where who you are intersects with what the company values, and those are the adjectives you use to create the perception that will be most valuable to *you*.

You must know how to make yourself relevant in any company and make sure you fit into the organization's product or profit equation. If people don't *perceive* that you have some differentiating factors, if people don't describe you using adjectives that are in line with the company's business model, then, chances are, you will just fade into the woodwork with the hundreds or thousands of others who haven't differentiated themselves. You will never be among the first to be considered for a promotion or a raise, and you will be passed over for key assignments. In the best-case scenario, you won't be very successful, and in the worst case, your days are numbered.

This is not to say that if you go through this exercise and choose adjectives that both establish who you are and what the company values that everyone is going to love you. The corporate environment is no different from any other environment where you have people working together—some people will decide, for whatever reason, that they just don't like you, and sometimes that's just the way it is. Still, this should not impede or discourage you from successfully executing your professional agenda, as I discussed in Chapter 2.

If you have chosen your three adjectives and attempt to line them up with adjectives that influence your success at the company or adjectives that the company values and you realize that there is no match, then it is time to reevaluate whether you are in the right seat, in the right department, at the right firm, or in the right industry. If you find that there is a clear mismatch, it won't be long before your performance and your career satisfaction will be compromised. If this is the case for you, should spend the next twelve to twenty-four months learning what you can from the company that you are currently working for to help leverage you into a different opportunity within or outside of the firm.

YOUR ADJECTIVES WILL CHANGE OVER TIME

As you become more and more senior in your organization or in your career, the adjectives that you want people to use to describe you when you are not in the room and the perception that you want to exist in the marketplace should change over time. When you are a junior person, you want your colleagues and bosses to think that you are eager, enthusiastic, and engaged, and that you possess the basic skills to do the job and are resourceful and analytical. As you reach midlevel in your career, you want people to perceive you as a good manager, someone who can get things done and who can mobilize others' efforts; at this level you want your firm to start thinking that you have foresight and the potential to think more strategically. As you become more senior, you want people to perceive you as visionary, commercial, and client-focused; and an authority on your subject matter.

Your adjectives will change over time, because what is required to be successful at each level will change, and frankly you will change and grow as a professional. There are expectations that exist at every level of seniority in an organization, and there are *perceptions* that exist about what a person at the level should speak, act, and look like. At first you must choose your adjectives to integrate with the expectations and perceptions that exist for the level you're at, while working to add to or change those perceptions as you grow and succeed.

As a managing director, there is an expectation that I will be able to influence client thinking, win business, and forge long-term relationships. While earlier in my career it was important to me to be perceived as tough, analytical, and quantitative, for example, today in my role as a managing director, I want to be perceived as tough, commercial, and a relationship builder. And I clearly need to demonstrate that I can do that, so those adjectives are a part of what I try to reinforce in everything that I say and do. However, it is still important to *me* to not just be known as a tough manager, but also a fair manager, because I now have people working for me. I want them to feel motivated to give me their best and to know that I will support and promote them.

CARLA'S PEARLS

- You can change the way people think about you simply by changing the way you behave, the things you say, and the words you use when you are speaking to them.

- Create a perception about yourself—build your own personal brand—by choosing three adjectives to describe yourself. Make sure you walk, talk, and behave consistently with those adjectives.

- When choosing your adjectives, make sure they are consistent with what the company values, but also make sure your adjectives are consistent with who you are and who you want to be.

- If you find you aren't in the right job or industry, spend some time thinking about what you are good at and what you would like to do. Then spend the next twelve to twenty-four months learning what you can obtain from the company that you are working for and what you can leverage to use as a stepping stone to your next position or industry.

CHAPTER 5

THE MENTOR, THE SPONSOR, THE ADVISER
Having Them All

Since the beginning of my professional career, the popular business press consistently has cited the need to have a mentor as a prerequisite to professional success. Over my many years of public speaking, I have given more speeches than I can remember on this topic. The questions that arise afterward generally reveal that most people do not have a realistic or correct definition of the mentor's role and its importance in the success equation.

While I agree that having a mentor is a significant component in reaching your career goals, it is certainly not the *only* relationship that will contribute to achievement in your profession. In addition, sometimes people that you might consider mentors cannot truly fulfill the mentor roll and should be considered more as advisers to you. My personal experience has taught me that while mentors and advisers are important, there is another relationship equally, if not more critical to moving ahead in an organization—the sponsor relationship. So, what's the difference between a sponsor, a mentor, and an adviser?

Adviser=Someone who can answer your discrete career questions, those that may be isolated questions pertaining to your career but are not necessarily in context of your broader career goals.

Mentor=Someone who can answer your discrete career questions *and* who can give you specific tailored career advice. You can tell them the "the good, the bad, and the ugly" about your career and you can trust their feedback will be helpful to your career progression.

Sponsor=Someone who will use their internal political and social capital to move your career forward within an organization.

Now that you know the difference between an adviser, a mentor, and a sponsor, how do you get one (or if necessary more than one) of each?

THE ADVISER

People often confuse the mentor with the adviser. They are not the same! An adviser is someone who has the skills or experience to give you good, strong advice. They may work in your field or may have many years of experience in general across one of many industries. They have enough experience to give you sound advice on questions that you might have pertaining to your job in particular or on navigating the political environment in general. However, unlike a mentor, with whom you share the good, the bad, and the ugly details of your career, an adviser is someone you turn to for discrete advice. In other words, advice pertaining to an isolated question that you may have about some issue or challenge as opposed to advice and counsel that pertains to your career progression.

For example, suppose you are considering two different job openings. The adviser is the person you might go to ask for details about the job's content or how the position fits into the overall organization. You might ask for information regarding what positions the predecessors have moved on to to get an idea of where this job could lead; or you may ask them their opinion about what key factors are needed to be successful in the position. You would *not* ask the adviser their advice on whether or not you are suited for the job, nor would you necessarily divulge how this position fits into your future career plans. You also wouldn't reveal that you see the position as a stepping stone to something else you may want to do. Another example of the type of question you would ask an adviser is how to approach a particular assignment you've received or how to make an upcoming presentation the most effective. You can ask an adviser for advice on the best way to approach a colleague they may know or for an introduction to someone you want to have in your professional or personal network.

Advisory relationships can be internal or external. Internal advisory relationships are often informal relationships that are formed as you get to know someone at work, and result from, a recruiting relationship, for example, or perhaps you work together in the same department. You adviser also may have been assigned to you by the company as a mentor as you start your career.

External advisory relationships are often those that you seek out on your own. They can form naturally out of a close personal relationship or can be with someone with whom you have developed a relationship over a few years. These relationships can include friends, former professors, headhunters, and people who have worked in your industry for a while.

If there is someone you admire and you believe they have the skills, experience, and a network that can be useful to you and from which you can learn, then it would be appropriate to begin an advisory relationship with that person. You don't always have to formally engage someone to be an adviser or mentor. You can wait until the relationship has progressed a bit and then seek to give the relationship a definition or title. Over time, as you continue to ask them for advice and engage in conversation, you will get to know each other better. Then, if the advisory relationship is successful, you can perhaps form the type of trusted relationship that eventually can develop into a true mentoring relationship.

THE MENTOR

There have been times during my career when I have not had a mentor, particularly when I was just starting out. Over the years, however, after a few tough experiences of painfully having to figure out challenges and craft solutions on my own, I sought the help of more experienced professionals, both inside and outside of my industry—I sought the help of a mentor.

A mentor is someone you rely upon to give you good, tailored developmental career advice. And note that I differentiate between developmental career advice and just simple advice. A mentor should be someone you trust, someone who gives you advice that augments your business learning and helps you to identify and navigate the politics of your environment as it pertains to you. The advice must be tailored, meaning it must be in context with who you are, what is important to your professional agenda, the skills that you are trying to attain, and the platform that you want to acquire. A mentor supports your professional development and provides you with the necessary tools to help you to improve your skills in a particular position or as a professional in general.

A mentor is someone you can tell "the good, the bad, and the ugly" facts about your career to and at the same time, someone who will give you the honest and unequivocal "good, bad, and ugly" feedback about your performance, your strategies, or your behavior. Your mentor has to be someone you feel comfortable sharing your vulnerabilities with, someone you can tell all the details of a terrible career mistake, if that's the situation. They have to be someone with whom you know for certain you can share information that won't be repeated someplace else.

For a mentor to be truly useful to you, before they can give you the best professional advice, perspective, or feedback, they must know *all* of the facts about where you are in your career. They need to know all of the details regarding the challenges for which you are asking advice.

Because the mentor/mentee relationship is so personal, you have to rely on your gut and instincts regarding the level of trust you place in this person. If you don't feel comfortable honestly sharing all of the dimensions of what is going on in your job with this person, **then they should not be your mentor!** You may instead want to consider them an adviser.

CHOOSING A MENTOR

The best time to get a mentor or a sponsor is when you are just entering an organization. Before choosing someone as your mentor you must already have an established relationship with them. In an ideal situation, a mentor will be someone from within your organization. You may have met them during the recruiting process or may have known them for a long time. Ideally *they* would take the lead in developing a mentoring relationship with you, shepherding your career and offering you valuable advice as your career advances.

In many corporate environments, mentoring relationships do not develop as easily for women, particularly women of color, as they do for men. Part of the issue is that mentoring relationships are more easily formed when there is some basic commonality between the people forming them—same gender, race, undergraduate institution, family background, religion, or extracurricular interests. In addition, in situations where there are several people with the same educational background, for example, but the parties are of different genders, the desired mentor is more likely to choose the candidate of the same gender. Remember, natural mentoring relationships are driven by what feels most natural, and we all feel more comfortable with people who look like us because we deem them to have more in common with us. I am not saying that you should not choose a mentor who does not look like you, nor am I saying that as a mentee you will not be chosen by someone different from you. In fact, I am a huge fan of having mentors who are different from you, whether it is another gender or race; I'm just saying that the natural process does not always happen that way. And if no one chooses to mentor you, then remember, it is *your* responsibility to find a mentor on your own.

So many people make the mistake of choosing a mentor only because they respect them professionally or because they are senior in an organization. These are, of course, very important criteria. However, if they don't really know you as a person and have some sense of who you are as a professional, they cannot be an effective mentor to you. They may be able to give you advice on relevant topics and act as an adviser, but they won't be able to tailor their professional advice just for you because they don't *really* know you: your strengths, your weaknesses, your background, or the details of your career aspirations. An effective mentor will give you advice that is in context with all of these things and more. Your relationship with your mentor and the advice they give should be very specific to who you are and to the environment you work in.

Many organizations will assign you a mentor when you are hired because their intentions are to help you integrate smoothly, effectively, and quickly into the organization. This objective is very different from what you are really looking for in a mentoring relationship. It is *not* just about integration, it is about career progression and success maximization. More often than not, these assigned relationships don't work over time. Why? Because they are not built on a trusted, established relationship. These arranged mentorships are more characteristic of advisory relationships.

You should *not* share all of your mistakes, fears, concerns, or career strategies with the company-assigned mentor until you have developed a trusted relationship. If you are just starting a new job and you are assigned a mentor, use this relationship as an advisory resource. If the person is in your direct reporting line, you can ask them to help you learn key skills, introduce you to key people in the organization who are fundamental to your network, or give you insights into the politics of the organization.

If you feel that you will not be able to develop a true mentorship over time, continue to utilize your company-assigned mentor as a resource the organization has provided for you, but find someone you feel truly comfortable with to be your mentor.

Many successful advisory relationships naturally develop into mentoring relationships as trust in the interaction between two people begins to develop. If you want to transition an advisory relationship to a mentoring one, it is apt to take more of the mentor's time. You will want to be sure to ask them about becoming your mentor. The conversation may go something like this:

> I have really appreciated the great advice that you have given me thus far in my career, and I think that you could be extraordinarily helpful as I navigate these next couple of years in my career. Would you be willing and available to help me

as needed and act as a mentor? I believe that you know me very well and understand conceptually what I am trying to accomplish and will speak frankly, confidentially, and honestly with me.

This type of dialogue clearly states what you are asking for and your expectations. If the prospective mentor is not willing to provide what you need, this direct request gives them an easy opportunity to decline. If you have had a successful advisory relationship with someone and you approach that person about becoming a true mentor, do not be disappointed if they turn you down. Good mentors will only take on a few mentees. While they may have several advisory relationships, they will only have a finite amount of time to take a genuine interest and in-depth approach to someone else's career given their own career, family, and personal demands. If they decline a mentoring relationship, continue to stay close to them and seek out another mentor internally or outside of the organization.

Your personal mentor is just that, personal. You do not have to advertise to others who your mentors are, nor do you have to let your mentors know if you have another mentor. Who you have chosen to help guide your career is your personal business, unless you choose to expose it. People in the organization will know who your mentor is if you have been assigned one, but again, if a mentor has been assigned, I would treat that relationship as an advisory one until you can access whether you have built a stronger bond with that person and they can help guide you in your career.

The agenda should only be about you

Another important consideration when choosing a mentor is that you trust the advice they give is based on only one agenda item—Y-O-U! In other words, you must be completely confident your mentor has your best interests at heart and will give advice that is right for you.

I say this because it is human nature to draw from our own personal perspective and experiences when rendering advice to others. But a good mentor uses the *objective* lessons they've learned to help others. *They do not introduce their own personal bias or subjectivity in giving advice to a mentee.*

Here's an example. I once had what I considered to be a mentoring relationship with someone who had a long, distinguished, and well-respected career in investment banking, and whom I had known for over a decade. Over the course of our relationship, I approached this person from time to time for discrete advice (advice about a single issue) and therefore assumed we had a mentor/mentee relationship. This was obviously before I knew the difference between an advisory relationship and a mentoring relationship.

One day I asked my mentor for guidance about how to obtain an opportunity. I wanted a platform that would give me greater authority. I felt I deserved it, but it was clear that I was not being seriously considered for the opportunity. My mentor gave me very provocative advice about how to approach the organization about my desires—in fact, it was explosive! I knew instinctively that if I followed the advice and the action didn't work, it could have a very negative impact on my career. My mentor's advice was influenced by a recent interaction with senior people that had an adverse outcome. Furthermore, and more important, I knew deep in my heart that the suggested advice was something my mentor would never do! In fact, if the strategy was successful, my mentor would be the net beneficiary of my actions, and if it failed, my mentor would be unscathed.

As a mentee, you want the benefit of your mentor's experiences and knowledge, their twenty-twenty hindsight, and the revelations of how they would handle situations better knowing what they know now. Further, you want to receive this information as it is relevant to you and *your* situation. But your mentor should not give you advice that they would not employ themselves. And only you can be the judge of that based on your knowledge of and belief in them.

Ultimately I didn't follow the advice, and in my mind this changed the definition of my relationship with this senior level person from one of mentoring to one of advising. After getting what I thought was biased advice, from then on I only asked this person for discrete advice and no longer chose to share the broader details of what was going on in my career, especially not the good, the bad, and the ugly!

Note that I did not sever that relationship; I simply changed the way I interacted with this person. I am sure that they did not notice any significant change in my behavior toward them, for I continued to interact with them as I always had. I continued to converse with the person, discuss work-related issues, and asked for discrete advice. I maintained the relationship as an important one to me, but I changed its content. Just because someone has achieved a certain level of success in their career doesn't mean that you should blindly follow their advice if it doesn't feel right to you. If you take bad advice, in the end, it is *your* career that will be affected.

If your mentor gives you advice that you find extremely uncomfortable to follow, examine the source of your discomfort. If they are asking you to do something that is outside your comfort zone because you have never done it before or you feel insecure, then they are challenging you to stretch yourself, and you probably should follow the advice. If, on the other hand, they are advising you to do something that you think is wrong or could have severe repercussions (as in the example above), then you should go with your gut and not follow the advice. In that case, you may want to discuss it with your mentor—be honest that you feel uncomfortable with their advice and that you are not going to go forward with it. You should let them know you will deal with the consequences of inaction, but that you appreciate their honest, straightforward advice.

You have a role in the mentor relationship

If you are in a strong mentoring relationship, ideally you should touch base with your mentor eight to ten times a year. You do not have to talk every week or month, nor do you need to have face-to-face meetings. But your interactions should be often enough that the mentor has the recent, relevant facts and context about you as a person and as a professional. This way they can be responsive when you need advice or as challenges arise.

In my mentor/mentee relationships, where I am the mentee I make it a point to touch base with my mentors *at least* once every six to eight weeks, even if I am not seeking their counsel. It is important for them to know where I am mentally, psychologically, professionally, and personally so that they are best equipped to render relevant tailored advice when I do make a request for help.

A mentor/mentee relationship should be taken seriously and carefully nurtured. Your mentor is investing time, valuable information, and experience, and you should value that for the gift that it is. As a mentee, respect your mentor's time and experience and use both judiciously. If you are asking for the mentor's counsel on a certain issue, then you should, in most cases, follow the advice. If your mentor gives you good, solid advice and you do *not* follow it, you risk breaching the trust in the relationship.

How do you think your mentor will feel? They invested their time, shared their experiences to help you, and then you don't follow through. How apt or enthusiastic will they be about expending their resources and energy on your behalf next time? Let's say you have chosen a person to be your mentor because you believe they have relevant experience that can help you. You trust this person and have developed a strong relationship with them. Then take their advice, do what they tell you to do, and follow through.

In addition to following through, you must also *follow up*! When you ask your mentor to help you with a particular challenge, it is also important that you let them know that you executed on their advice and what the outcome was. In closing this feedback loop, you further underscore the importance of the relationship and demonstrate an appreciation for your mentor's investment in it.

Mentoring is one of the topics I am asked about most. Here are some of the most common questions:

"Does a mentor have to work for the same organization I do?"

I don't believe your mentor has to work for the same company you do, but I think it certainly is helpful. By having a mentor that works for the same firm, there is a better chance they will understand the environment you work in, what the culture is like, and who the players are. Working for the same firm gives your mentor a context for your questions and challenges. At a minimum, I think you need to find a mentor who understands the organization and industry you work in well enough to give you useful, relevant advice and professional guidance.

"What if my mentor betrays my trust and tells my boss something that I asked them to hold in confidence?"

First, you should understand *why* your mentor felt they needed to share the information. They may have exercised their professional judgment on your behalf and may have honestly felt that it would be in your best interests to share the information. Obviously a confidence is a confidence, and it should not have been broken. However, depending on the rationale behind sharing the information, you may or may not choose to change the nature of the relationship. If you are not satisfied with why your mentor shared the information, then be careful of sharing confidences in the future. If you are comfortable with why they shared the information or you are pleased with the outcome of the action, then do not change the way you are currently characterizing and treating the relationship.

"Can I have more than one mentor?"

Certainly I think that you can have more than one mentor. But at the same time, I don't think that it is wise to share the intimate details of your career with many people. Your career management and progression is personal, and the more people that you share the details with, the less able you will be to manage your privacy and your professional strategies.

If you are just starting your career or are at a new company and haven't entered into a solid mentoring relationship yet, consider having several advisory relationships. I am a big fan of having a board of directors type of strategy for managing your career. Essentially this means having various people you can call upon at different times for a variety of career needs. Your directors should be a diverse group, diverse in seniority, ethnicity, gender, and professional background. The more diverse your board is, the greater the breadth of advice and knowledge you will gain from it.

Your directors can provide you with invaluable help, particularly in the area of professional development and the softer skills you'll need, such as managing vertically, managing upward, managing

laterally, navigating the political waters, communicating effectively, positioning yourself for promotions, and building effective
relationships.

I've used this approach throughout my career, calling on certain
people when I had discrete questions about my professional area of
expertise, others when I wanted to approach my boss in the most
effective manner, and still others when I needed a quick jump-start
to my motivation or needed to regain focus on my goals. This
group includes peers, people who are very senior to me, and many
others who work outside of my area of expertise of investment
banking and capital markets. My directors each come from different backgrounds and industries. Some I have known for more than
thirty years and others I have known for less than one year. But the
one thing they all have in common is that they are honest,
no-nonsense professionals who are accomplished in their own right
and are willing to participate in my professional and personal advancement. In my opinion, those are the key criteria for putting
together an effective career advisory board of directors.

"What happens when a mentoring relationship goes wrong or doesn't work? Can I 'fire' a mentor?"

As you progress throughout your career, it is important to
keep in mind that your professional and/or personal needs will
likely change. Therefore, you should feel perfectly comfortable
changing mentors. The mentor who helps you in the early days
of your career may not be the right person to assist you in navigating the often choppier, more political waters as you advance
and become a senior professional. However, please be careful not
to abandon the relationship; most relationships that you forge
and take the time to nurture are relationships worth keeping.
You may not engage or invest as much as you did in the relationship when it was more relevant to your career progression, but

do *not* abandon it. You never know when you may need that relationship again or when you can do something for the person who invested in you.

In addition, your mentor's needs may also change and they may no longer have the capacity or the desire to commit the time and focus it takes to continue to be a great mentor to you. This is no one's fault and you shouldn't take it personally. You should continue to treat this relationship as important, but at some point you might begin to consider it an advisory relationship and perhaps look to find another mentor.

You should not look at your adviser, mentor, and sponsor relationships as merely strategic. You do not want to approach getting to know someone with the ulterior motive of getting something out of them. You should look at relationships as the important connector to climbing up the career ladder. In every aspect of your career, your relationships will be an important contributor to how you are viewed in the organization, when and how you move from one position to another, and your exposure to new opportunities. The adviser, mentor, and sponsor relationships will be key to helping you gain the skills and experiences that you need to be successful and to help you navigate the political landscape in your organization.

THE SPONSOR

In this chapter, I have spent a lot of time talking about mentors and advisers, but in my experience the most important relationship you can have in your professional life is a sponsor. In every critical decision about your career—promotions, compensation, important assignments—someone has to, as I like to say, "Carry your paper into the room."

The sponsor is the person who is an advocate for you behind closed doors, someone who argues on your behalf. The sponsor is responsible for presenting and arguing the case for *you*—for a new assignment, for a promotion, or for an excellent bonus or an increase in salary. Your sponsor is the person who asserts your position in the company. While they must be cognizant of your weaknesses, more importantly, they must be passionately focused on your strengths. This person must have the definite, positive point of view that you are a valuable asset to your team, department, and company. They should have adequate political and social capital within the organization to get things done, and, more important, they must be willing to use that capital on your behalf.

It is important to recognize that within the politics of every organization—and there are politics in *every* organization—not everyone who is qualified and who deserves to be promoted or paid well can be. There usually are more qualified people than there are opportunities available. This is simply one of the laws of the professional jungle, so to speak. If you are not chosen for the promotion or the pay raise at the time you think you are ready, you cannot take it personally.

In every organization, when there are important decisions to be made about assignments, pay, and promotions, someone is going to win and someone will lose. But one way to make sure you do not experience too many disappointments is to make sure you have a sponsor. Your sponsor's role is to make sure that the person who loses is not you!

In considering a sponsor, you must choose someone who has a position of power at the decision-making table. They must possess the political and social capital that affords them the respect and power within the organization to make things happen. You can discern who has a seat at the decision-making table and power to make things happen by carefully studying your environment.

Who has the authority to hire and fire? Who seems to have the last word in team meetings? If your company makes decisions by committee, find out who is on the compensation committee or the promotion committee to assess who are some of the powerful people in the organization. This information usually is not confidential. It is not widely publicized, but it is not confidential. If you do not have a mentor who you can ask, be proactive and ask the person who recruited you or someone in your department who is slightly senior to you.

More important than having a position of power at the decision-making table, the sponsor must be willing to expend some of their capital on your behalf. Ask yourself, "Why would anyone spend their capital to support me?" "Why do I deserve it?" and "How do I make the case that I am worth their investment or expenditure?" More importantly, ask, "If my sponsor helps me to obtain my objective, what's in it for them?" The answers to these questions will affect your sponsor's decision to expend (or not) their capital on you and will be central to their arguments supporting your case behind closed doors.

It is particularly important to have a sponsor in an organization that relies on a committee structure for decision-making regarding promotions, compensation, and new opportunities, as is the case in most financial services environments. In a committee environment, generally someone will have to expend political capital in order to push an agenda through, unless the committee is unanimous in its opinion on a topic. This is an extremely critical point in understanding the laws of the corporate jungle. It is costly every time someone has to spend political capital. There is a trade-off, one thing for another.

If your sponsor argues on your behalf for a promotion, bonus, or assignment against opposition, then they probably will have to offer something to the opposition to get their support. Sounds a lot like Washington politics, right? It's not that different. You probably will never know what the trade-off is for your sponsor, but you need to make sure that the benefit to your sponsor for getting you what you want is well worth it in their eyes. If you are a candidate who has widespread support throughout the organization and it is time for a promotion, then perhaps your sponsor's expenditure will not be so expensive and you could achieve your goal without a lot of pushing from your sponsor. On the other hand, if you have moderate support—no one is really pounding the table on your behalf but you have no real detractors—without the added support of a sponsor your promotion, pay, and assignment very easily could stall or die inside of a committee decision-making structure. In this case, your sponsor will have to spend capital in order to push your agenda through the committee. And it probably will be costly. If they are not willing to spend the capital on you, then you will not get your promotion or higher bonus or be selected for the new opportunity.

Now that you know how important a sponsor is, how do you get one?

The best time to think about identifying a sponsor is when you are contemplating joining an organization or when you are being recruited for a specific job within the company. After you have received an offer of employment, ask yourself, "Among the people I have met, who will be personally committed to making sure that I succeed?" "Which of these people are in positions of power or can introduce me or connect me to someone who has a seat at the table?"

If the answer to that question is not obvious to you, then before you take the offer, start to socialize and ask the question of the people who are most keenly focused on trying to get you to join the company. The conversation can go something like this:

> I am really excited about joining X company and I think that I can really make a contribution at the outset and over time. However, we both know that success within an organization does not solely depend on our contribution and performance. It also depends on having someone support and sponsor us as we move through and upward in the organization. Someone has to be committed to our success. Given all of the people I have met in this recruiting process, who can I count on to be committed to my success? Who will sponsor me in the organization? Will you be a member of my success team?

Obviously, you only want to ask the last question if you are speaking with someone in the organization who you have already identified as a person with a seat at the table, who appears to have a lot of political capital and who might be willing to consider spending some of that on your behalf. It is prudent to at least have the foregoing conversation with all of the key people you are meeting as you are being heavily "sold," or persuaded to join the organization.

If after you ask the question of several mid-level and senior people within the organization, you still don't have an answer, reconsider whether you really want to join that organization. It is imperative that upon joining a new company you have at least two people you believe you can count on to sponsor you in those early days in your new assignment. And make sure that you literally get their commitment to sponsor you; don't just assume that they will. Even if you are changing divisions or jobs within the same firm, you want to make sure that you have that sponsorship going in, particularly if it is a large company and you cannot depend upon the sponsorship from your old job (that sponsorship now *has* to go toward supporting your colleagues who are still within that area). Finding a sponsor *after* you've taken a job is often harder to do. But don't despair. If you're already working for a company and have yet to recruit a sponsor, here are some tips and characteristics to look for:

A sponsor must have power in the organization

Your sponsor must have a seat at the decision-making table and a voice of authority in the room where the table resides. This is an important point. It is not enough that your sponsor has power within the organization; they must be respected *and* have a sphere of influence in the environment where you are looking for action.

Let's say you are looking for a promotion from associate to vice president in the investment banking division of a financial services firm. The most effective sponsors for you would be a senior managing director in investment banking and one in your direct industry or product area. They could make personnel comparisons and speak directly to the impact you have on clients and revenue or your market and product knowledge. Their word is, therefore, likely to carry more weight with other decision makers around the table.

In that same example, if your sponsor is, instead, well respected in the asset management division but doesn't have strong allies or is not a part of the decision-making process in the investment banking area, the bottom line is that your desired promotion could be at risk. While this sponsor's arguments will be respected, they are not likely going to be viewed as equally valuable as the arguments from a sponsor in the same functional area. If there is no one at the table from your division who is willing to exert influence on your behalf, you could be in trouble.

Ideally, your sponsor should be your boss. But that does *not* always have to be the case. In an environment where decisions are made in a committee structure, your sponsor can be anyone on that committee. However, you will still likely need a supporting voice from your direct boss. If your boss does *not* have a seat at the table, then you need to have a strong relationship with someone from your functional area who does, and your boss might serve as a conduit or a bridge to that relationship.

Similar to our discussion about attracting a mentor, nirvana is when a sponsor chooses you. The sponsor may have recruited you into the company, may have trained you, and may be your current boss. This obviously is the best of all possible worlds because your boss, for example, is likely already professionally and emotionally committed to your success. They have identified you as a dedicated hard worker who adds value to the company or the department. They think you are someone who could be of critical importance to the company in the future and they want to be a part of the team that helps you succeed.

However, the scenario of a sponsor naturally seeking you out is often not the case for women, particularly women of color. In many corporate environments, a boss may have several people within an organization they should sponsor but may only have enough power to really make things happen for one or two people and not the four or five who need and deserve sponsorship. Again, if you are not one of the people chosen, don't take it personally. If it is apparent that your boss is not a clear dedicated sponsor, it is your responsibility to take the lead in identifying and developing this important relationship with someone else or asking your boss directly. Sometimes you simply have to ask someone to be your sponsor.

Back in 1999, when it was time for me to get my critical promotion to managing director, I asked myself, "Who will be arguing on my behalf in a crowded room of others who are advocating for their candidates who, like me, also want to be promoted?" I quickly realized that I could not confidently answer the question and identify who would be passionate about arguing my case over someone else's. I therefore concluded that my promotion was at risk.

Do you see how critical this point is? The reason my promotion was at risk was not because I did not have the right credentials or that I didn't work hard; it wasn't because I hadn't earned a promotion. My promotion was at risk because I had no one at the decision-making table who I knew, without a doubt, was passionately committed to arguing my case, someone who felt it was their personal responsibility to champion my promotion over other candidates who also had the right credentials and deserved to be promoted.

Once I realized my vulnerability, I approached a senior managing director who I knew had a seat at the decision-making table. His voice was respected and I thought he would consider being my sponsor. My speech went something like this: "It is very important for me to get promoted this year and I need someone on the promotion committee who can argue for me. Specifically, I need you. You are in the best position to advocate my candidacy because you have seen my work, heard client feedback, and know that I am ready for this position. I know that you could do a superb job on my behalf. I will make sure that you have the strongest package possible on me when you walk into the room."

Now it's safe to say that he was somewhat taken aback and probably inclined to say no. I had, however, presented such a logical, honest argument that I was hard to say no to. He agreed to fill that vital sponsor role for me. I also found someone who did not have a seat at the table, *but* who was a passionate advocate for me and who was a key influencer of the other important players in the room. They also acted as a sponsor for me with other decision makers around the table and helped my chosen sponsor achieve success on my behalf.

You might think it was a very risky move for me to ask this person to be my sponsor, but from my perspective, I had nothing to lose. He would either say yes and agree to be my sponsor, and I would trust him to keep his word, or he would say no, in which case he would have to tell me why he declined my request. Either way, I would gain something very valuable. If he said no, I would gain valuable insight regarding why he did not think my candidacy should be supported, and perhaps why the organization might not support me. And in the event that he agreed to be my sponsor, then I would be fairly certain that he could get the job done, and he did.

Ultimately, to successfully move forward in your career, you'll want to have both a mentor *and* a sponsor. Nirvana is when you have them both at the same time and they both work within your organization! However, for most of us, things do not always work out exactly the way we plan. Most likely you will have one or the other at different times in your career.

You certainly can be successful for a period of time without having either, and you can do fairly well for a while without a mentor, but finding long-term success within an organization is nearly impossible without at least a sponsor. You *have* to have a sponsor. Ask yourself this question today: "Who is carrying my paper into the room?" If you can't answer the question, stop working so hard, get up from your desk, and go recruit a sponsor!

You can't just get; you also have to give

Every good relationship is a two-way street and the adviser, sponsor, and mentor relationships are no exception.

Consider your sponsor. They are benefiting you by using their political and social capital to help you achieve your objective. But, in return, they will want to know, to use an investment term, what their ROI, or return on investment, will be. In other words, what will they receive in return for their expenditure of their capital on you?

Professionally, the ideal return is the credit or the increase in power they'll receive by being associated with making something, such as a promotion, happen for you. Remember, everybody loves a star, and everyone wants to have the most respected and talented people in an organization on their side. If you are considered to be a star in your organization, it gives your sponsor more power and credibility because they are now associated with *your* team by virtue of your success.

For example, if your sponsor is still fairly young and is perceived to have many years left at the firm, your continued success and rise through the company further empowers their team of supporters and loyalists, and their power base of support continues to grow. If a sponsor steps up for you, there is an implicit and an explicit understanding that you will be there to return the support at *any* time.

I am not suggesting that you are beholden to your sponsor for *anything* that they might ask. There are limits. I am suggesting that you should understand that your sponsor used political and social capital on your behalf and you will be expected to spend some of yours to help them or someone else. You should never do anything that would compromise yourself professionally or that you do not believe in. If you are asked to do something for a sponsor that goes against your beliefs, then you should politely decline, but actively seek to do something else that could be helpful to your sponsor. For example, suppose your sponsor asks you to support an internal candidate for a promotion or a specific task, but you fundamentally do not believe that the person is the right one for the job. Remember that your ultimate responsibility is to add value to your company. If you do not feel that the person will add value, then articulate this to your sponsor and seek to do something else for them that they might find valuable.

People say to me all the time, "Well I'm just a junior cog in the wheel here; I can't give anything back to a mentor or sponsor." You would be surprised at what you might hear at the junior level that might be interesting for someone in a senior position to know or what skills or knowledge you might have that could be useful for your senior sponsor to learn.

You may have access to relationships that could be helpful to your sponsor, even if you are at a more junior level. For example, I once was pitching an important piece of business and one of my former mentees now worked at the firm that could award us the business. While he was not the ultimate decision maker, he was very close to the senior person who was making the decision. After the meeting, he gave me valuable feedback that my team could use in our continued quest for the business. He also continued to speak favorably to his boss about our track record and ability to deliver what we pitched, and he could speak personally about the integrity of the team. We were chosen as one of the book runners (the managing or lead underwriter who maintains the books of securities sold for a new issue) on the transaction, and I am confident that my mentee's efforts on our behalf were an important determinant.

As a junior person, your relationships, information within your peer group, and even your perspective can all be very useful to a senior person. In the relatively flat environment of financial services, particularly in investor institutions, people with junior titles can wield a lot of power and influence internally. If you are that junior person, you can use that power to enhance, influence, or reciprocate an important sponsor relationship.

Information is power. I'm not suggesting you break trusts or share confidential information. But thinking about how you can add value for your sponsor or mentor will create a mutually beneficial relationship you both will want to nurture for years to come.

CARLA'S PEARLS

- An adviser is someone who can answer your discrete career questions, those that may be isolated questions pertaining to your career but are not necessarily in the context of your broader career goals.

- A mentor is someone who can answer your discrete career questions *and* who can give you specific tailored career advice. You must trust the person you choose as a mentor enough to tell them "the good, the bad and the ugly" about your career, and trust their feedback will be helpful to your career progression. To find a mentor, consider choosing someone who has had a lot of experience in your industry and who is approachable enough to begin an advisory relationship. Remember that your mentor does not have to be within your company but should have some familiarity with your industry, the political environment, and the prerequisite skills needed for you to succeed.

- A sponsor is someone who will use their internal political and social capital to move your career forward within an organization. While it is important to have a mentor, it is equally if not more important to have a sponsor. A sponsor is your advocate. They are the person who, behind closed doors, is responsible for presenting and arguing your case.

They are cognizant of your weaknesses but are passionately focused on your strengths. They have a position of power at the decision-making table and possess the political and social capital that affords them the respect and power within the organization to make things happen for you.

● Think about creating a board of directors to help you manage your career. It should include advisers, mentors, and sponsors. Your directors should be a diverse group—diverse in seniority, ethnicity, gender, and professional background. The more diverse your board is, the greater the breadth of advice and knowledge you will gain from it.

● Like any other relationships, in order to be successful, the mentor and sponsor relationships have to be mutually beneficial. It can't be just about what *you* get. No matter what your level of seniority, there are things you can offer your sponsor or mentor to help them in their careers, too.

CHAPTER 6

LEVERAGE YOUR VOICE
Articulate Your Views and Your Expectations

One of the most important keys to maximizing your professional success is exercising your voice. Everyone within an organization has a voice, but the difference between those who do really well and those who do not is this: Those who do well understand that they have a voice, they identify it, and they use it. They use their voice to underscore their relevance in the organization.

Why is relevance important? To be relevant in any organization means that you matter. If the organization cares about who you are and what you are working on, then it considers you to be valuable to the organization. If you are considered to be valuable to your organization, then you are by definition on your company's success track. Your voice is what helps to define your relevance. It is true that there is a direct correlation between your job function or your job content and its real relevance in a company. In other words, if you are the person who has primary responsibility for a major revenue-generating account in the firm, then you are going to be considered quite relevant to your firm as opposed to someone who is very removed from the company's core business model and revenue-generating capabilities. But your voice is what you use to define and articulate the importance of your job, change the content of your job, or redefine your job. Your voice is what you use to get an opportunity to prove yourself. Your voice is what will help you get a well-earned promotion. It is not enough to perform the tasks that you think will earn you a promotion; you must also ask for it. You must use your voice to make it clear to the company that you have earned it and expect to get it. Your voice is what you use to articulate your views, goals, and expectations to the firm.

Exercising your voice in any organization does three things for you. First, it creates a perception about who you are and your role within an organization. Second, it creates a level of expectation within the organization regarding your contribution. When you share your ideas, opinions, and expertise, people come to expect to hear what you have to say. You want the company to be conditioned to think of you as a contributor. Third, it creates a mechanism by which *you* can define your expectations of the organization.

USING YOUR VOICE TO CREATE A PERCEPTION

Remember the story I told you in Chapter 1 about the well-respected, high-ranking woman who wondered what was wrong with me because I would sit in meetings and not speak? While I certainly was a very smart, hard-working member of the team, she had no way of knowing it. I have always been vocal, even outspoken, but obviously somewhere along the way, in my first couple of years as an associate, I had lost my voice. I was inadvertently and unconsciously creating a perception of me that could have severely impaired my career progression.

What perception was I creating by not exercising my voice? I was creating a perception of being someone who was shy and demure, someone not cut out for the hard-driving business of finance. Of course, this could not have been further from the truth. How was this woman or my clients supposed to know that I was magna cum laude from Harvard University in economics and that I had attained second year honors at Harvard Business School? How was she to know that I had very strong quantitative skills, and that I was a quick thinker and solution oriented? I do not wear any of these attributes on my sleeve, so how was she, or anyone, for that matter, supposed to know unless I exercised my voice, demonstrated my intelligence, and used my verbal contributions to underscore and support the perception that I wanted to create?

My silence was creating a perception that was putting my reputation in jeopardy. I had fallen on the wrong side of what I call the 50/50 rule. The 50/50 rule means that when people meet you for the first time, before you ever speak, there is a 50/50 chance that they think you are smart and a 50/50 chance that they'll think you are stupid. These perceptions are, at least in part, created and destroyed by how you express yourself verbally, how you use your voice. If you are trying to move up as a professional in any environment, you can't afford to passively accept those odds and risk that people in the room will think you're stupid simply because they never hear you say anything. By not exercising my voice, I was not only missing an opportunity to add value to the organization, but I was also creating a perception that could have sunk my career.

I see it happen over and over, especially to otherwise smart and capable women. I am not sure if these women think that it is safer or lower risk to appear nice and quiet, than to risk saying something in a meeting that could be challenged or perhaps shot down. I also believe that women often tend to think, "I am not going to say anything, Preston just said what I was going to say," or "What Bettye said is very close to what I was thinking; I don't want to be repetitive." But whatever the reason, before you know it, you have gone through an entire meeting, or several meetings and have not said a word. And this is the wrong approach. It is through your voice that you allow people to hear what you have to offer and learn who you are.

How did I lose my voice? I was working for someone who was considered very tough and not good to work for, and I had had a couple of experiences that did not go well. I was beginning to doubt my ability to succeed within the organization, at the firm broadly, and perhaps in investment banking in general. I would argue that my confidence had been busted, and instead of taking the lessons from the mishaps, I was starting to become tentative, fearful, and unconfident. When we are not confident in who we are, we start to doubt what we know and we tend to become quieter and retreat from expressing ourselves in the organization. We stop exercising our voices. This less than confident demeanor creates a definite competitive disadvantage and will derail you from the path to success.

Not only did I start to retreat from active, verbal participation in team and client meetings, but I also gave away an enormous amount of power by not using my voice to tell someone that things were not working out well with the person I was assigned to. Even though *that,* in fact, was the single biggest reason things were going awry for me. Instead, I did what most women tend to do—I suffered in silence and boy, was I miserable!

There have been many studies conducted and many articles written about how most women typically leave an organization, because of a bad boss or several bad experiences. They start to feel isolated or alone because of those experiences and perceive that there is no one they can talk to about it. In most cases, they do not exercise their voice to change their work assignments, the people that they are working with, or the content of their job. Instead, they stay quiet about the situation, continue to suffer in silence, and eventually leave the company. In some of these cases leaving the organization may have been the right call, but in other cases, the situations could have been changed or corrected, and these women wouldn't have had to interrupt their career flow and begin over again at a new firm. Not exercising their voice created a competitive disadvantage of time and start-up costs in a new environment that may have been avoided. Saying something to someone, exercising their voices, could have affected change for them.

HOW TO USE YOUR VOICE

Now let's talk about *how* you use your voice. While it is important to speak up in an organization, how you use your voice is also a key skill. If you want to create a certain impression, you should strategize about what you want to say and how you want to say it. You create a perception about who you are, not only by speaking, but also by how you speak. Think about the perception that you want to create and then use words that will support it.

For example, if you want people to think that you are analytical or quantitative, then you should incorporate numbers into your language. When someone asks your opinion on something or why you used, for instance, certain assumptions in a model, you would want to answer something like, "There are three reasons why I think . . ." or "I used five key assumptions when building this model." If you want people to think you are creative, then say things like "I like to think creatively, so I tried to incorporate a few out-of-the-box ideas when developing this solution," or "This problem called for creative thinking, since this is one of the toughest challenges we have seen yet, so I . . ." By using this type of language, you set the listener up to think of what you are saying within the framework you have defined. If you do it repeatedly and reinforce it with your actions, they will come to see you in the way that you have defined. Remember Chapter 4 and our discussion about perception? In exercising your voice with the right words, you can sway others toward thinking you are smart by presenting intelligent and compelling ideas.

Think actively about *how* you want to use your voice. Do you want to use your voice to be constructive or to complain? Do you want to use it to be supportive or to be contrarian? Do you want to interrupt people all the time or be the one who summarizes the discussion after every meeting to exhibit that you were not only listening, but also to have the chance to put your own spin on what was said? The way you use your voice can be an important factor in influencing your relevance in an organization. How you use your voice will be a key element in reinforcing the perception that you want to create about who you are, where you belong, and where you want to go in the organization.

CREATE A LEVEL OF EXPECTATION WITHIN THE ORGANIZATION

The more an organization hears your voice, the more it will expect and want to hear your voice. When people have become conditioned to think that every time you open your mouth it will be value add, then they will look forward to hearing you speak. In order to create this expectation, make sure when you do talk that your comments are relevant, timely, intelligent, solution-oriented, or containing key facts. By conditioning an audience to expect a certain contribution, they will seek you out more and more to hear what else you have to say.

I can't emphasize enough how important this is. If you find yourself in a situation where you are not speaking, then know that the perception that exists about you in the organization is that you aren't contributing. If that's the case, then I have two words of advice—say something! If you can't think of anything to say that you think is relevant or important at first, then in your next meeting, paraphrase someone else's comment. Move a preposition and a noun, and simply rephrase what someone else has already said. Men use this tactic all the time, with great success! You have to start to get your voice into the room. If you don't start, you can't practice. If you don't practice, then you won't get good at it.

I am not saying you have to speak constantly. Nobody likes a windbag, the person who feels they have to dominate every discussion or conversation. But the more people hear your voice, the more comfortable they become with your voice, and the more they will want to hear your voice and seek you out to find out what you have to say. As a result, the more relevant you become. It is so easy, especially in big companies, for you to get lost and fade into the woodwork with the hundreds of others who don't speak up. You don't want that to happen. If you become irrelevant in an organization, you become more expendable.

Making your voice heard may not always be easy at first, particularly when you are in a new job or at a new company or you are a very junior person in a room with important, senior people. If it is not natural for you to speak up in group interactions or to present in front of large groups of people, you must practice by doing it. The only way that you will improve and get comfortable is to do it over and over again. You may make mistakes and it may be a while before you feel comfortable, but you will get more confident in hearing your voice and in positioning it in a way that it can be most effectively heard.

It is particularly important, especially for women, to talk with authority and confidence when we speak. Remember, particularly in a corporate environment, you are selling yourself first, your skills, performance, or the facts about you second, and your judgment third. If the listener hears or perceives that you are not confident in what you are saying, then they immediately will discount you and everything that you say or do afterward. If they doubt you, they won't trust you, and they will start to seek out alternative sources of information and people they believe they can depend on. This is not an outcome that you want, in relation to your internal interactions with colleagues or with clients.

When I was a third-year associate, I was traveling with a woman senior to me at the time, and she said, "Carla, your main problem right now is that you are too willing to show it when don't know something. You are way too honest about that. When you appear unsure of a fact or an answer to a question, people start to doubt that you know what you are doing. Let me share with you a little secret that 'the boys' taught me early in my career when I was a young associate: Frequently Wrong, but Never in Doubt. It means that you always answer with confidence even if you don't know the answer. Show no doubt, even if you are wrong."

Whoa! I was stunned and couldn't believe what I was hearing! There was even an art to saying I don't know! I thought that I was showing that I was even more sure of myself by being confident enough to say I don't know when I didn't know the answer. Instead, I was undermining my credibility by expressing doubt. As I began to really test what she said, as I observed the environment, I realized she was right. I noticed how people senior to me would react to unexpected queries in meetings with clients and internal colleagues. I remember one meeting in particular when a very senior person gave an answer to a question. I knew that he didn't have the correct answer because we had not prepped the question in our premeeting, but I had the data with me and could answer. Before I could interject with the appropriate answer, he had rendered a response that was not entirely correct. Still, though, he had answered confidently and authoritatively. His answer was not questioned and was accepted enthusiastically as gospel and I was not about to contradict him. Later in the meeting, I weaved the correct information into the dialogue without exposing either of us.

What did I learn? It was not *what* he said, but *how* he said it that made all the difference. The lesson for me was not that it's okay to give wrong information, but that it is important to speak with confidence if you want credibility within your organization or you want to build trust with clients. If I am not sure of an answer, I will confidently render one anyway and leave myself room to adjust or change the answer later.

The response typically goes: "In my judgment, the answer is _____, _____, and _____, but I will double-check a couple of sources and get back to you." Or "My experience tells me that the answer is _____; however, let me check with my colleagues to assess if there is an alternate point of view." My answers reinforce that I have a perspective drawn from my experience that establishes some credibility but leaves room for the answer to be improved or changed. This approach demonstrates more confidence than saying "I don't know" or "I am not sure" alone, particularly when it is a new relationship and you are trying to establish credibility to deepen it. It is also important that in speaking confidently, you speak audibly. Most people tend to speak quietly or softly when they are not confident in what they are saying. I can always tell when someone in a meeting is unsure of their answer because the decibel of their voice starts to decline or starts out low, barely audible.

You shouldn't be surprised if when you do talk, people try to distract you. In highly competitive environments like financial services, there are certain people who love nothing better than to try to intimidate and distract you and mute your voice just for fun.

When I was starting out as a first-year associate, some of the guys I worked with would smirk at each other and make these funny faces and furrow their brow every time I said anything. It was as if to say, "What is she talking about?" or "That doesn't make any sense." I would get very self-conscious and start to think, "Am I not speaking in English? Did I conjugate a verb incorrectly or something?" It was really intimidating, and I started to become afraid of speaking up. I started to lose my voice.

But then I started to realize it was just one of the games played in highly competitive environments, kind of like a fraternity hazing to try to trip me up, so to speak, to see what I could take, to discourage me from speaking. If they were successful in executing their tactic, then the outcome would be that I would start to shrink from contributing in meetings or speaking in group settings. And then I would become more irrelevant to the environment and certainly less competitive with them. Beware of these kinds of tactics. If it happens, don't be intimidated. Don't clam up! Simply find someone in the room who is your supporter and look at them while you talk. If there isn't anyone, just pick someone and stare back at them no matter what kind of face they make and keep talking, confidently.

I eventually learned my own tactics. In fact, I not only figured out that using my voice was powerful, but I also discovered that silence can be very powerful, too. After I earned a reputation for being an active participant and speaking up in meetings, sometimes doing a little eyebrow lifting of my own when certain people talked worked very well. In fact, when I was quiet for a long time or didn't comment on something, people noticed.

They'd say, "Carla, you're quiet, what are you thinking? You look like you don't agree." You'll find that when you have a voice, silence can be a significant tool as well. Then, when you aren't speaking, people will want to know why and you'll hear, "Kay, what are you thinking?" Or "Anthony, how do you feel about that?" As you get more experienced, you'll learn when it's best to speak and when it's best to just sit and be quiet.

An ancillary benefit of creating an expectation that you will exercise your voice is that it deters people from treating you unfairly or trying to put one over on you. Most people are fairly nonconfrontational and will not create a situation they think will create a public altercation. If you have a reputation for speaking up for yourself, other people are less likely to try anything dishonest or unscrupulous with you because they know you won't stand for it and you'll say something.

USING YOUR VOICE AS A MECHANISM TO ARTICULATE YOUR EXPECTATIONS

As I mentioned before, I often joke that I am a graduate of the "You Don't Ask, You Don't Get" school. I have learned the hard way that it is your responsibility to manage your career. (See also Chapter 2.) Part of that management means articulating to the organization your expectations. Too many of us are under the illusion that if we keep our heads down and work hard that things will all work out as we wish. Unfortunately, it is not that simple. Everything I have talked about in this book contributes to maximizing your success; one other important element is stating and asking for what you want. Whether it's in terms of promotions, pay levels, or new assignments, letting the right people know what you want for your career is imperative to getting it.

My eureka moment came one year when I did not get promoted to the next rank on time. It was a tough year on Wall Street. I had done moderately well in terms of pay and bonus, but in tough years on the Street, everything gets cut back—compensation, promotions, and the like. I had not said a word all year about wanting a promotion, but I had continued to work hard and expected that all would work out in the end; of course I would get it.

Well, in the end, I did not get promoted that year and I was really upset! I waited a few days (until I calmed down) and then went to talk with my boss. After I expressed my displeasure and disappointment, he calmly said to me, "Carla, I was wondering when you were going to come and talk to me. Your peers have all been in and out of my office for months now pleading their cases. I never heard from you. Unfortunately, we had to make some tough choices this year. Why didn't you speak up? Didn't you know that we are the captain of our own ship?"

Wow! He blew me away! In that one moment I realized how my failure to exercise my voice, to articulate my expectations, had put me on the wrong side of a marginal decision. You must understand that sometimes, particularly during tough market environments, promotions, new assignments, and compensation decisions, while extremely important, sometimes are made at the margin. That means that not everyone can get promoted every year. Not everyone can receive top pay. And sometimes the final decisions within your organization can come down to the margin, down to two people who are equally qualified, but both can not get promoted or paid well. The person who has made their voice heard has a better shot of ending up on the right side of the margin *every time*. I could no longer be angry at my boss or the organization for what had happened. Instead I was grateful to my boss for sharing the truth with me and giving me such a valuable lesson regarding the importance of exercising my voice.

Your voice is not only important to help you communicate in meetings, but it also will help you articulate your career goals as well as what you expect to receive in the way of opportunities, promotions, and compensation. There is an old adage in the sales and trading business that says, "You have to ask for the order." Women, especially women of color, must understand that to receive the order you have to ask for it.

I understand that for some people this approach feels counterintuitive to how they are used to doing things. Many of us, especially people of color, are raised to believe that the opposite of speaking up—working hard and keeping your head down—is the way to success. I am here to tell you it is not. I like to say, "Keeping your head down doesn't keep you from getting shot; it only increases the chances that you won't see the bullet coming!"

Especially in difficult environments, such as when there are layoffs, management changes, and other corporate shake-ups, keep your head up. Look for opportunities and speak up! It is never the people who keep their head down who are saved during chaotic times. In bad economic periods, for example, companies are looking for out-of-the-box ideas, ways to make money and cut costs. Speak up, share your ideas, and then follow through on them. People often say they are going to do something but never do. When someone comes up with a good idea and then takes it a step further by following through on the idea, they differentiate themselves and are admired and rewarded. Don't be afraid to put forth your ideas and your expectations. Keep your head up and exercise your voice!

One of the questions I'm often asked is, "When do I let them know my expectations?" The very best time to have this kind of conversation is within the first quarter of beginning a new job or assignment. Once you have oriented yourself to a new position, within the first month is a good time to sit down with your manager to discuss the path that you are taking for the rest of the quarter, the next six months, the first year, and so on. Most of us do not do this. We don't feel comfortable having this conversation at the outset and think waiting until our first evaluation is a better time. The risk in waiting until then is that during that first year, you potentially could miss some important guidance from your boss that could be helpful to you in creating the organization's perception about you, or for learning important facts about the company. Having the conversation early in the year gives you the opportunity to get insight and information from your boss on how to move forward.

Once you do get to the formal evaluation, it is a great opportunity to exercise your voice in articulating your expectations of the organization. Many people see their annual or semiannual performance evaluation as a one-way conversation. You sit and listen and your manager talks. The manager reports on what you did well over the last evaluative period and what you need to improve on. This is the wrong approach! It is important for you to be an active participant in the evaluation process. You should focus the discussion on the triumphs, defeats, and needed corrections in your performance over the last year, with the goal of focusing on the three or four things that could take your performance to a higher level. Remember, only a third of this evaluative conversation should be focused on lessons learned regarding your past year's performance and lessons that can be used to leverage into better performance, more responsibility, and greater authority. Two thirds of the discussion should be focused on your aspirations for the coming year.

Before your meeting, consider what *you* want to accomplish over the next twelve months. What skills do you need to learn?

What types of transactions or deals do you need to be exposed to experientially? Do you want a promotion? Do you want to take on bigger, more complicated assignments? Do you want a chance to work overseas? Or in another division? Whatever your desire, express what you would like to happen in your career in the next twelve months. It is perfectly fine to talk about longer time horizons, but it is most constructive to talk about twelve-month intervals, which is the normal evaluative cycle in most companies.

In addition to talking about what you would like to accomplish in the next year, you should also talk about what you need from the organization to be successful in those endeavors. If you need help from your manager in getting exposure to certain types of assignments or people within the organization, enlist their pledge to do so. If you need certain training, ask them for a commitment of resources and a timeline in getting it accomplished. Never set a goal, particularly in your evaluation, without a timeline. You have twelve months until the next evaluative cycle and you should have a three- to six-month timeline to achieve most of the objectives that you develop on your evaluative report card. Let your manager know what kinds of support you need from the organization and from them specifically to help you make your goals happen.

Let's say you expect to be promoted next year. Then you should ask for your promotion *this* year. You should have conversations with your manager and supervisors letting them know your goal in enough time to clear up any skill or experience deficiencies. If you wait until near promotion time to have this conversation, then you might hear responses such as, "You are not ready because you haven't achieved this level of sales or had exposure to this type of product," or "You haven't managed enough people on your platform," or "The job you have is not one that will get you promoted to the next level." If you wait too late to get this feedback, then you are too late to apply corrective action.

Exercising your voice to articulate your expectations is a no-lose proposition. Either the organization will confirm that you are on track for your promotion, strong bonus, or whatever you're looking to achieve, or it will tell that you are not. Either way you win; if you get what you want, great! But, if the organization says no to what you ask for, then they will have to tell you why, and that is valuable information to have. This way you have data that will either allow you to improve or that will help you make decisions about what you should do going forward. You will also know if you won't be able to accomplish your career objectives within that particular organization. They'll either say, "Keep doing what you're doing," which is a vote of confidence and reassurance that you are on the right track for success, or they may stammer, make excuses, or say they aren't sure, which means you could be vulnerable. If this happens, then it's an opportunity for you to start a dialogue to see what you need to do or change to reach your goal. If you are not on track, this conversation can help you develop a strategy to get there.

Because you had the evaluative conversation and you used it to lay out your plans, goals, and expectations for the next twelve months, you now have a *report card* to follow, a list of your goals and the steps you must undertake to achieve them.

ONE CONVERSATION ISN'T ENOUGH

Over the next twelve months, you can use your voice as a tool to follow up. Every few months (I recommend every two months) with your manager either formally or informally proactively sit down and have a conversation about your progress. Say something like:

> You told me I needed to do A, B, C, and D to get promoted next year. Well, I just want to let you know I've completed A and B, and expect to have C and D completed by this date. What do you think? Is there anything else I need to work on? Is there anything else that I need to do to make your job easier in sponsoring me?

Let the company know how you are progressing, discuss any challenges you are having, and ask for feedback on what you have accomplished so far. Speak up, start the conversation, ask for what you want, and then work to reach your goal. Have whatever tasks you need to accomplish to get promoted, or whatever your goal, checked off on your report card within six months. Check in with your boss formally at the six-month mark. Use your voice to reinforce what you've done. Whenever you get the opportunity, talk to your manager and other people who may influence your promotion, and drive home what you've accomplished. Remember, you are driving and managing your career. It is your responsibility to ask for what you want. When you need a reminder to ask for what you want, remember that the Good Book says, "We have not because we ask not," and you immediately will have the courage to ask!

This will also give you the opportunity to discover if there are any problems or issues. If there are, you'll still have plenty of time to fix them before your next formal review at the twelve-month mark.

DON'T JUST TALK, LISTEN

Let me caution you, be careful to make sure your evaluation is a true two-way discussion. You can't just talk. You also have to be open to receive constructive feedback. While the evaluation shouldn't be a one-way street with your manager doing all of the talking, it also shouldn't be you defending every point they make.

Getting feedback can be very valuable. It offers you a chance to improve and enhance your skills and behavior. But if you approach your performance evaluation defensively, you will impair the communication, shut down, and create an environment that is not conducive to giving or getting feedback. I am talking especially to my African American sisters when I say this. Because we can approach an evaluative discussion, especially one we think might be difficult, with "that look" on our face, and it makes other people uncomfortable. I am not saying this face doesn't sometimes come in handy. But in a professional evaluative environment, the other person is simply going to be put off. And to avoid a difficult conversation or a confrontation, they won't be honest or specific, and you won't get the truth about your performance.

If your colleagues or superiors think that it is going to be a difficult experience to give you feedback, then they will not give it to you. You may get gross general statements like "You are generally improving," or "You are performing on par with your peers," or "Like everyone else, there are a few things that you need to do improve," but you will not receive the hard, concrete feedback that would allow you to build a detailed roadmap for improvement. You will receive watered-down versions of the truth that may sound okay, but will not allow you to fix the right things and move forward. In the end, you won't get any useful data, and you need that data to improve.

I know about this from personal experience. One of my colleagues shared with me that my boss had once said, "I hate giving Carla feedback because she has an answer for everything.

She always has something to say." He was right. At the time I felt that I needed to defend myself against feedback that not only wasn't true, but was rather perfunctory and negative. I felt that I couldn't let unsubstantiated comments hang out there in my evaluation because they might create a *perception* of truth in my boss's mind. If he felt, however, that because of my defensiveness, he could not talk to me, then this wasn't a good situation for me either. If he avoided giving me constructive or even complete feedback, particularly feedback that could have been difficult for me to hear, but nevertheless very useful to me, then I was never going to get anything truthful from the conversation. How then could I ever really know how I was viewed or how I could improve my skills and advance? I wasn't opening the door for him to truly help me or creating a safe environment for him to honestly speak to me.

I shared this information with a mentor, a colleague I trusted, and she gave me some great advice. She told me, "During your next evaluation, no matter what he says, you say yes or uh-huh and nothing else." Now, let me reiterate, as I mentioned before, I have a reputation for speaking up and telling the truth, even when the truth is something people don't want to hear. But I took my colleague's advice and I did it. And let me tell you, it was *sooooooo* hard to keep my mouth shut! Especially because this manager had a tendency to just take what other people said about me at face value without questioning it, and much of it just wasn't true!

But I did it anyway. To everything he said, I simply replied, "yes" and "uh-huh." I threw in some "Oh reallys? Okay" and a few "Yes, that's interestings." After that meeting, he told that same colleague that I was open, that I listened, and that I was "quite constructive." By not being as defensive or *perceived* as defensive, I had created a nonconfrontational environment where he felt like he could give me honest feedback. He felt like he could tell me the truth and I would accept it in the spirit in which it was intended—to help me. And as a result, although I certainly did not agree with everything he said, I did learn some constructive, detailed information about my performance and how to improve, which is the only way to successfully move forward in your career.

I also learned about the power of listening, about being open to communication rather than focusing on being right. Sure, I did not feel that *every* thing he said had merit, but by listening to him, I communicated that I cared about my performance, I cared about what he and others in the organization thought of my performance, and, more importantly, that I wanted to do whatever it took to correct anything that I needed to and outperform. In following through on the advice, I now also had a strategy on how to communicate with my manager that would serve me well going forward.

From then on, the feedback he gave me was not only constructive, but in ensuing conversations we were able to have real two-way dialogues that were extremely helpful to both of us. He went from being just a manager to also being an adviser and eventually a sponsor. And unlike before, when someone made a comment about me that wasn't true, rather than just accepting it, now he said, "Oh, I haven't seen any evidence of that." He would discount the statement and move on. He was now a member of my success team. By the time he left the company many years later, he was one of my biggest supporters!

Part of exercising your voice is being willing to listen and to use your voice constructively in a conversation. When you are willing to accept that others have something to offer, when you are willing to accept feedback and consider that you aren't always right, you give yourself the opportunity to grow. If you approach a meeting expecting that the other person is looking to get you, to find something on you, it won't be productive. If they are determined to find something on you . . . so what? Let them! Be willing to listen to what others have to say, have the courage to be honest with yourself about what you've heard, and then use what you learn to your advantage to help you move forward. Think about *why* they might be against you, why they aren't a member of your success team, and what you might be able to learn in that conversation that might change that. And don't forget to say thank you. Let people know you appreciate them and value what they have to say. Even when you hear something you'd rather not hear, they are giving you a gift, a chance to become better than you were before.

Obviously, I am not advocating being a pushover. I am certainly not saying you shouldn't exercise your voice when you need to. I am saying not to be defensive and learn to use your voice at the right time, even if someone gives you feedback that you don't wholeheartedly agree with. Here's an example: Someone once said about me, "She doesn't know the convertible product," an important product in the equity capital markets area. It wasn't true. In fact, they had no way of knowing if I knew about it or not. I had not yet worked on any deals with them involving the convertible product. People sometimes just make statements to have something to say, without regard to whether it is true or not. It's annoying, but it happens in corporate life. Rather than getting defensive, I simply replied, "Of course I know it. But I haven't had a chance to demonstrate that. I welcome the opportunity to show it." And then I made sure I knew everything there was to know about convertible products. Because after that, I knew for sure someone would test me to see if I really did know it and I wanted to make sure that my statement was supported. When you have the chance to correct or debate something erroneous that someone has said about you in an evaluation and demonstrate what you know, you'd better be ready.

The bottom line is, make sure the organization hears your voice. They need to know that you are smart and capable, and they also need to know what your expectations are. Especially in larger companies, there are a lot of employees just like you. You have to remind people that you've come to build a career and that you expect to be rewarded for performance, that you plan to get promoted and paid well. If you do not exercise your voice on your own behalf, then who will? If you don't tell the organization your expectations, then you have to assume that they do not know them and that they won't likely be fulfilled.

CARLA'S PEARLS

- Speak up. Don't sit quietly in meetings and say nothing. Your colleagues and clients won't know if you are really smart, or, worse, they might assume you don't have a clue. Even if you just rephrase what someone else has already said initially, it is important for people to hear your voice.

- Using your voice does three things: It creates a perception about who you are, it creates a level of expectation about your contributions to the organization, and it creates a mechanism by which you can define your expectations to the organization. Don't be distracted by tactics people use to intimidate you into remaining quiet. They are just games people play.

- Sometimes silence can be just as valuable a tool as speaking up. Use both.

- Use your voice to be an active participant in your evaluation. Ask for what you want. "Ask for the order."

CHAPTER 7

HAVE A PENCHANT FOR TAKING RISKS
You Can't Go Wrong

If you want to get ahead in life or in business, the bottom line is that playing it safe won't get you there. Many of the world's most famous and successful people have talked about the importance of taking risks in order to move forward in life. The actor Alan Alda said,

> Be brave enough to live life creatively. The creative is the place where no one else has ever been. You have to leave the city of your comfort and go into the wilderness of your intuition. You can't get there by bus, only by hard work and risk and by not quite knowing what you're doing. What you'll discover will be wonderful. What you'll discover will be yourself.

And the great writer and poet T. S. Eliot said, "Only those who risk going too far can possibly find out how far they can go." And Robert Kennedy, U.S. attorney general and 1968 presidential candidate, said, "Only those who dare to fail greatly can ever achieve greatly."

When you consider almost any successful person you know, I will guarantee every one of them has taken some kind of risk to get to where they are. Some have taken the risk to leave positions where they were comfortable and considered the leader in their field to take on positions where they had little knowledge or experience and where they potentially could have failed miserably. Some have taken the risk to boldly ask for the positions they currently have, and that was a risk, because they could have been told no. In fact, they could have been pushed out of their old positions because someone might have interpreted their asking as a signal that they weren't committed to or interested in their old position. Some have taken the risk to move from one firm to another and taken on much greater responsibility or positions of authority. And still others have made bets on introducing new and innovative products that required tremendous amounts of initial funding capital and have in the end made significant profits for their company. The bottom line: In order to be successful in any corporate environment, you must take risks.

I would argue that in today's dynamic, fast-paced corporate environment, the proliferation of information and technology has somewhat leveled the competitive knowledge landscape; and what differentiates you is your willingness to take risks. I believe this to be the success equation for most corporate environments:

Achieving Success and Moving Ahead = Performing Extremely Well + Aligning with Internal Politics + Taking Risks

THE LULL OF THE STATUS QUO

Interestingly enough, most people avoid taking risks especially professional risks whenever possible. The longer you are in a job, the more comfortable things get. You are going along, you like your boss, the work is okay, and you've had a pretty good career so far. Maybe you think about taking things to the next level, expanding your department, or trying for that big promotion, but why stir things up? Why put at risk what you've worked so hard to build? Most of us think, "It was a competitive process to get this job. I am getting paid relatively well. What happens if I take this risk and it doesn't work out?" Then the clincher is "I am not sure that I can get another job like this one—maybe it's not worth the risk?" Once you start to let fear enter the success equation, then you will avoid taking risks and thereby underpenetrate your opportunity for success. It is that kind of fear-based mentality that subconsciously puts us in the frame of mind where we avoid taking risks and as a result delay success.

Especially in today's highly competitive marketplace, the "same ole, same ole" just won't do. The technology boom has made almost every industry dynamic—things are constantly changing. Companies spend an enormous amount of human, financial, and technological capital trying to figure out the next generation of a product or process, often before they have released the current version. If you are content with doing things in the same way that they have always been done, then you are likely going to become misaligned with the company's forward strategy to maintain its competitiveness. If you're doing your job the way your predecessor was doing it, you, too, will likely soon find yourself a predecessor.

You have to approach your job with the mind-set of, "How can I make my role better? How can I make my job bigger? How can I add more value to my assignment, to my team, and to the company?" Whenever you do something different or venture into uncharted waters, you are, by definition, taking a risk. But it is the only way to heighten your potential for success.

I am not suggesting you become a renegade making reckless decisions and taking actions without thought and preparation. There's a big difference between taking risks and doing things that are just not smart. When I talk about taking risks, I am talking about three types of risks: calculated risks, studied risks, or "step out on faith" risks. With each type of risk, you must think through the objective (what you are trying to accomplish), the actions (the steps that you have to take to realize the objective), and the consequences (what can happen positively or negatively as a result of your actions). Remember what you learned in high school physics class: "For every action there is a reaction."

Doing something not so smart would be to take a risk without any thought of the potential consequences; where a bad outcome could mean, for example, that you lose your job when you are not financially or emotionally prepared to do so. That is not risk taking; that is, well, just not smart. If you are certain you will regret the outcome of taking a certain risk, then the choice is clear—don't do it, end of story.

CATEGORIES OF RISK

But before we talk about types of risks, let's backtrack a little and talk about categories of risks. One of the other reasons many of us don't take risks is that we fail to embrace risk taking as a part of our equation for success in our jobs or careers, and that we don't know how to properly categorize or evaluate the risks we need to take.

In my mind, there are two categories of risk: latent risks and forward risks. *Latent risks* are risks that exist every day in your career. They are not directly tied to your performance, who you are, or what you do. These are risks that are out of your control. You wake up one day, turn on the radio, and hear that your company is a takeover target. Management and the board of directors decide to sell off certain assets, one of which is your division—that's latent risk. Your boss, who is one of your outstanding sponsors (see also Chapter 5) decides to leave abruptly and you no longer see a clear path to promotions or opportunities to moving forward—that's latent risk. Your company asks you to take on a new job, one that is inconsistent with your skill set, power bases, or interests, and you fail miserably. And, by the way, you don't have emergency financial resources or a strong professional network to act as a security net—these are all examples of latent risks.

Each of the aforementioned situations occurred without any impetus from you, yet each situation affected you and could mean a marked, even detrimental turn in your career.

How do you prepare for latent risk? The truth is, you really can't. But what you can do is compensate by always looking to find the second category of risks, *forward risks*. Forward risks are risks that *you can* take to potentially positively affect your career. They are actions for which you cannot 100 percent predict their outcome, but you can be 100 percent certain that by taking them you will be better off with respect to your skill set, experience level, finances, or positioning yourself for an opportunity outside of the company. Just the act of taking the risk, whether it works out well or not, leaves you better off, because forward risks move you ahead in your career endeavors.

In order to maximize your success, you should always seek out forward risks. If you are actively seeking out forward risks, then you are by definition looking for ways to improve, looking for ways to be a greater value add to your company, and you are therefore positioning yourself for greater success. You can't always anticipate latent risks, nor should you be preoccupied with them. Instead, you should spend your time actively thinking about and taking forward risks whenever you can. In Chapter 2 I talked about being the architect of your own agenda. Seeking and taking forward risks will enable you to improve and accelerate that agenda.

Consider Hannah. She was a very successful lawyer and partner in a large prestigious law firm. She was approached by one of the firm's most important clients to work for them as general counsel. Hannah had worked hard for the partnership in the current firm and finally felt that she had the power and respect that she deserved. The new opportunity offered great upside potential. The general counsel position was her dream job. In her previous position as outside counsel for regulatory issues, she focused on a discrete set of legal of problems. In her new job, with her firsthand exposure to the company's business model, in three to five years she would be positioned to become a COO, or even perhaps a CEO. At a minimum, the new general counsel job offered her an opportunity for exposure to more varied legal issues.

In Hannah's mind, the path to taking on the opportunity was fraught with risks. If she made the move, she would have to integrate into an entirely new and very different culture. Suppose she didn't fit? Suppose the politics were too voluminous and intricate for her to quickly become adept at playing them? If she failed, she probably couldn't come back and resume her current partnership seat, or could she?

For Hannah, this was a risk worth taking; it was a classic forward risk. In going for the opportunity, Hannah would be better off, no matter what the outcome. If the opportunity works out, Hannah gets her dream job as general counsel and is exposed to even bigger opportunities within the company. She can also maintain relationships at her old firm by negotiating that she be the person responsible for interacting with her former company. She could use her current strong relationships at the new firm (we are assuming that they are strong, otherwise they would not have offered her the job) to quickly learn, navigate, and integrate herself into the new culture, thereby maximizing her opportunity for a smooth transition and entry into the politics of the organization. If, for some reason, things did not work out at the new organization, Hannah still wins because now not only does she have the experience of general counsel on her resume, she is now a more attractive candidate for other general counsel opportunities, *as well as* for partner positions at other law firms.

Over time, as you seek out and take more and more forward risks, you eventually will land a position of power and authority and then as latent risks arise, you will have a platform and experience from which to navigate them and move your career safely to protective waters.

CALCULATED RISKS, STUDIED RISKS, AND "STEP OUT ON FAITH" RISKS

So now that we've established the two primary categories of risk, let's discuss the three principle types of risk I mentioned at the beginning of the chapter the calculated risk, the studied risk, and "step out on faith" risks.

Calculated risks are ones for which the pros and cons of taking an action are very clear and the action itself, the thing (or things) you need to do or say are crystal clear. With a calculated risk, again, think physics—for every action you can accurately predict the reaction. You are clear on the range of consequences that can transpire if you take a calculated risk.

Carrie was up for promotion for senior vice president. She felt strongly that she had been ready for at least two years, but the organization had not yet promoted her. She knew her immediate boss respected her work, thought that she was terrific, but that either he did not have the power to push her promotion through on his own or he was not being effective in arguing her case in front of the promotion committee or the committee director. Carrie knew it was important for her to be promoted *that year*. Otherwise she felt she would have to leave the organization because she had maximized her potential and her performance in her current seat. She was concerned that if she continued to stay without being promoted, she might jeopardize her attractiveness as a candidate when she began to seek other external opportunities.

Carrie knew it was time to mobilize to action. Her objective was to communicate to her direct boss and his boss that she deserved and expected a promotion, and that it was important that it happen in that year. The action Carrie took was to set up two separate meetings, first with her boss's boss. Then she met with her direct boss and told him what she had done and why. The potential outcomes? Carrie's boss could be angry that she had the conversation with his superior without his knowledge. Or he could respect the fact that she felt comfortable and confident enough to have the conversation on her own and was respectful enough of his role to make sure that he was informed. Other potential consequences: the senior boss could be angry and not be supportive of her because Carrie approached him directly. Or he could have gained even more respect for her since she behaved like a senior person and approached him on her own behalf. Carrie also was fully aware that if her plan did not work, it would be time to seek opportunities externally. But after carefully considering the risk and all the possible results, she was prepared to do that if necessary.

Carrie had taken a very calculated risk. She had clear objectives, she knew the appropriate actions to take, and she was very aware of all of the potential consequences. She took the risk, and she got the promotion!

Taking risks for which you can see what action needs to take place but where all of the consequences are not immediately clear is a studied risk. Say you need to ask someone for help or support with a project but you cannot anticipate their reaction to your request. Perhaps you don't know the person you need to approach well enough to anticipate their answer. Or maybe you don't completely know the internal political landscape enough to anticipate the fallout or repercussions of your actions. Perhaps you want to give a client advice that you know may be counter to what they want to hear or what is most commercial for your firm at that time. But you know that it is the right advice for the client, and if they take your advice, it might be a bridge toward strengthening your relationship with them. A studied risk identifies the action to be taken but does not reveal all of the potential reactions that may result or may not fully anticipate all of the subsequent actions that might be necessary.

Toward the end of the first technology bubble, I was working with an Internet company to execute its initial public offering (IPO). The company had completed the road show and we had a book of demand (potential investors), but we had not received much feedback from accounts regarding the work that they had done, the valuation, and the ultimate positions they desired to hold. This is the kind of information you normally receive from investors when they are really, really interested in investing long-term in a company. While we clearly had a book of demand, even an oversubscribed book of demand, my gut was telling me to recommend to the company and their parent company, that we postpone the transaction. My concern was that the market did not feel stable, that the buyers may have just been placing an order to be in the flow of an Internet transaction, most of which had gone well so far that year. They seemed to lack conviction in the company and appear to be committed to being long-term holders of the stock. If I was right, the stock would not trade well after the deal was priced and it would be a catastrophe for the company, the parent company, investors, and for our franchise as well. But how do you tell a company that they should not price when there is a book of demand?

To advise the company not to price the deal clearly was a risk. The client could have become angry, forced us to price the deal, and then decided never to do business with us again. I could have taken serious criticism at work for postponing revenues. And a competitor could have stepped in and taken the business away while we were waiting to return to the market a few months later. Or taking the risk could result in a positive outcome: The client could take my advice, appreciate my boldness in giving them the "right" advice, and waited a few months to return to market and complete a successful transaction.

This was clearly a studied risk. I knew the objective: to price a successful transaction for the company, one that would trade well in the market after it was priced and maintain a strong relationship with my client. I recommended that they wait and price the transaction in the fall, when, hopefully, the market would have a better tone and buyers would be more apt to add new names to their portfolio. The company took my advice and did not price that day. The next day, when the stock would have started to trade, the NASDAQ was down over 100 points, and almost of all Internet companies that were priced on that day traded poorly. In fact, most of them traded below their IPO price. The company was happy they waited. They took our recommendation to price the deal a few months later and when they did, it was a success.

While I clearly studied and weighed this risk, I could not clearly anticipate what the outcome or the consequences would be. Nor was I completely prepared with a plan of what I might do if I received a lot of criticism for making this gutsy call to not only postpone revenue but potentially to lose it all together if a competitor came along and took the business. I made the call, however, because I believed the upside of gaining trust with the client and executing a successful deal for them outweighed the downside risks of an internal career setback. Because you cannot anticipate or accurately predict all of the outcomes of studied risks, the upside has to be markedly greater than the downside if things go awry.

"Step out on faith" risks are those for which you can identify the outcome that you want to achieve, but you are not sure of *how* you are going to make it happen. For example, you may know that it's the right time for you to start a business. The market for your product or service is teeming, you have a pipeline of potential customers, and you have lined up suppliers, but you don't know whether the business will have the initial momentum it needs to make it successful. There is no way that you can anticipate or project potential demand. You therefore decide to move forward (forward risk) not knowing exactly *how* you will make the venture successful. You step out on faith and trust in your abilities, taking the risk without fully understanding how you'll do it or the potential range of outcomes.

Now, I am always the first one to say that, "with God all things are possible." But I also believe in the old adage, "God helps those who help themselves." That means you should think through, as carefully as possible, all of the risks you want to undertake and their potential outcomes. When you are managing risk in a corporate environment, you want to take as many risks in the forward and calculated risk category as possible. There are too many interdependent players in the game for you not to have a handle on what the potential outcomes of your actions might be, as is the case with step out on faith risk. There are your superiors, your subordinates, your peers and colleagues, and your customers or clients, and, therefore, many potential combinations and permutations of reactions from these people to every action that you take. If you want to maximize your success in an organization over time, you must seriously consider each of them. There always will be a time and a place in your career for the step out on faith risk, but you should try to limit those types of risks to the times when you are the primary person affected by taking the risk and the repercussions on or for others are very, very small.

Stephanie was an internal development coach for a large technology firm. She developed a unique model and process to help employees to develop leadership skills and to figure out ways of making a greater impact on the organization. While she liked her job, she felt somewhat stagnant. Stephanie was ready to make a much bigger impact than she could within her company by bringing her new coaching model to employees all over the country. She did not know how or if she would be able to attract other large corporate clients, but she believed her approach was unique and far better than other training modules she had seen at other corporations. She put together a business model and decided to leave her job to start her own coaching business. It was a big risk. She was well thought of in the company, considered one of its rising stars. She walked away from a steady six figure salary, benefits and other perks. But her risk paid off, and today Stephanie is CEO of her own company, her former company is a client, and she coaches employees from coast to coast at some of the most prestigious firms in the world.

As you endeavor to take risks, particularly in trying things that have never been done before, such as opening up a new market, creating a new product or process, or starting a new business, you will encounter people who tend to be negative and will try to project their negative views onto your endeavor. These people will be happy to suggest all of the ways that your project could fail. Do not let them stop you. No matter what you do in life, there are always going to be plenty of people who can come up with count-less reasons why you shouldn't _____ fill in the blank! Why you shouldn't try A or B because know one has ever done it before, it's too risky or too hard. Let their advice be just that, a negative view, and don't let that stop you from taking a risk.

THERE IS NO DANGER IN RISK TAKING

It is my belief that there is never any real danger in taking well-thought-out calculated risks. In my many years on Wall Street, I've never seen anyone who has taken a risk that hasn't eventually paid off for them. No one I know who has ever stepped out and taken a risk later turned around and said they regretted it. In fact, it's usually the opposite. Most people look back and regret *not* tak-ing a risk. They realize now, with more experience and confi-dence, that they would have survived no matter what the outcome. Perhaps the risk may not have seemed to pay off at the moment; in fact it could have been a bad move at the time, but they always saw the benefits come to fruition later.

At the end of the day, the thing that stops us from taking risks is fear. Whenever I find myself hesitant to take a risk, I remind myself of that old saying: F-E-A-R stands for False Evidence of things Appearing Real. In other words, what you fear doesn't re-ally exist. We generally are the ones who create our own obstacles or barriers to moving forward. There really isn't a downside to risk taking. What's the worst that can happen? You'll fail. So what?! **Failure always gives you the valuable gift called ex-perience.** Take the lesson, learn from your mistake, and move on. If you think of yourself as a leader or you want to be one, you cannot operate on fear.

If you are fearful of your surroundings and your standing in the organization or that you don't have the appropriate abilities, you will project that to others and be dismissed as irrelevant in the organization. Furthermore, you will find yourself stagnant, almost paralyzed in the company. You will become complacent and rote in your actions. You will in effect create a competitive disadvantage for yourself and will not be considered for new opportunities or greater authority because you are *afraid* to try new things, to move forward.

Inevitably when I say this at a speaking engagement, someone from the audience will raise their hand and say, "But I am just a junior person, I don't feel it's my place to step out and take certain risks." First of all, as I talked about in Chapter 1, your level of seniority doesn't dictate your importance to the organization. You were hired by the firm because you are a smart, capable person. Whoever hired you saw from your résumé, your recommendations, and the way you presented yourself, that you had potential to add value to the company. No matter what your level of seniority or your position, you are an important part of the organization and you should conduct yourself with that in mind. A part of that mind-set includes consistently asking yourself, "How do I make what I am doing better? How can I make my platform bigger? What risks do I need to take to make that happen?"

Therefore your title, whether you are very senior or very junior, shouldn't influence your thinking in terms of what you can and can't do, particularly as it relates to taking risks. For example, if you are a first-year associate in investment banking, your official job description is likely to include assisting with client presentations. You'll be responsible for doing background research on the client, making initial statistical analysis, running valuation models, identifying comparable companies for valuation analysis, and drafting transaction marketing materials. No one tells you whether it's okay to call a client directly without permission from someone on the team if you need clarification on something. And nowhere does it say that you should hang back, keep quiet, and not participate in meetings. There are plenty of things that you can do to showcase your talents that are perfectly acceptable, valuable, and that will demonstrate your ability to be proactive and highlight your leadership skills.

When I was a first-year associate, I put many unnecessary limitations on myself. I thought because I was a junior person, there were only certain things I was allowed to do. No one told me that they were just restrictions I had placed on myself, restrictions that I had created in my own mind. It was hard, especially when I was starting out, because I didn't have the background or a prototype for what was considered acceptable. This is not unusual, and is particularly true for women and people of color in corporate environments. We are often the first pioneers in our families to hold the types of positions we have. We come to the table highly educated, from the top schools, with extensive skill sets, but then we put limitations on ourselves and define our jobs in very conservative terms. We think, "Oh, I'm just starting out, I'm a junior cog in the wheel, it's not my place to say too much or to try to make any major contributions. I'll just keep my head down and work hard, and once I get myself established and have a higher position, then I'll start doing things to step out of the box."

But the exact opposite is the case. The only way to get to that higher position is to step out of the box early! A friend of mine once gave me excellent advice about risk taking. He told me that it's easier to beg for forgiveness than ask for permission, take a risk. And it's so true.

What does that mean? It means that it's better to step out and make a mistake than it is to sit around and wait for someone to tell you it's okay to try something new. If you think you need someone else's permission to take a risk, think again. If you are trying a new idea, implementing an out-of-the-box solution, there is no precedent or protocol. So why would you need to ask someone else's permission?

Trust me, if you step toward what's considered over the line, someone will be more than happy to tap you on the shoulder and let you know to step back. But when you ask other people's permission to do something you've empowered them to do so simply by asking the question, even if they don't necessarily have the power to tell you how or what to do.

You are in your seat today because you have the intelligence and ability to do the job extremely well. So you are quite capable of coming up with some new way of thinking that might differentiate you from the pack of folks who are attached to playing it safe. You've come up with an idea, weighed the pros and cons, you've done your research, you've talked it over with your mentors and your sponsors (see also Chapter 5), and you've decided that, while a little risky, you believe this new way is the best solution. Then there's nothing left to do but to do it! You must act!

I once heard Meg Whitman, former CEO of eBay, say something that I found very profound: "The price of inaction is greater than the cost of making a mistake." And she's right. This statement illuminated for me the power of taking risks and the price you pay for not taking them. If you do not move forward, go into uncharted territory, you will not stretch, learn, or grow. So then how can you maintain your competitiveness and maximize your success? If you continuously embrace risk taking, chances are you'll be promoted politically and economically, and both are very important.

Take the risk. And if it doesn't work out—you make a mistake and maybe step on a few toes in the process—you can always say, in the most professional and gracious way, "I am so sorry. I didn't mean to do it." If you had a good plan and your intentions were honorable and in line with the company values, you may get a little egg on your face, so to speak, but you will come away with something incredibly important—the gift of experience. Now you know how to do it better and differently in the future. And you've had a taste of the direction you want to go in.

THE RISK IN MAKING CHANGE

There is a risk in making a change, whether it is taking on a different job, or moving to a different division or even to a different firm. It's scary. You wonder whether it will be the right move. One way to evaluate the risk of change, taking on a new job or assignment within a company, or moving to a new job outside of your current employer, is to use these risk metrics. Ask yourself the following three "test the waters" questions:

1. Is this new opportunity going to give me skills and experience I would not have if I stayed in my current position for the next twelve months?

2. Will the new position expose me to people and relationships that I would not otherwise be exposed to if I stayed in my current seat for the next twelve months?

3. Will the new job create new branches on my decision tree of opportunities going forward that will give me more choices after I leave the new position at some time in the future?

If the answer to all three questions is yes, then the new job—the change—is a good risk to take. Whenever a change could result in a positive outcome for you, then the risk is worth taking and the change is worth making. Many people fail to make changes in their careers because they become blinded by the potential negative consequences and do not assign the proper weight and importance to the positive outcomes of the risk.

I have seen many people make the mistake of not taking on new opportunities with more power, authority, and a platform with the potential to accelerate their career trajectory, because they were being offered the same compensation to do a different, more responsible job. Their argument was "I'm not being paid more, so why should I take on more responsibility?" They failed to realize that the new opportunity was a platform that could be used to argue for more money and more authority once they occupied the position.

I have also seen people fail to embrace the change of going to a new firm because they were afraid of the political risks, unsure of integrating into the new culture, or afraid of not performing at the level expected by the new employer, even if the compensation was significantly better than at their old firm. In this case, it was a risk worth taking because they were being compensated to take the risk of a new environment and political landscape. In addition, the new opportunity gave them the chance to further enhance their skill set, which would create new career opportunities when that job or experience had run its course.

THE RISK OF SAYING NO

While in most cases, change is a good thing in your career, there are times when the risk of change may be greater than the upside of doing something new. There can also be a level of risk in not taking opportunities that may arise for you—the risk in saying no.

One of the most important risks that I ever took in my career was to turn down a new opportunity that my boss asked me to consider. It was the same year I was up for a promotion to managing director, and I was asked to start up a new effort in capital markets focusing on retail investor distribution. However, I loved my syndicate job and knew I was really good at it. I was responsible for marketing, pricing, and distributing public equity transactions. I instinctively knew that I would have a stronger and longer track record from which to get promoted by staying where I was than to have only six to nine months of experience in this new endeavor. I also knew that if I declined the job, I ran two risks. One, that my boss might be annoyed with me and not sponsor me for a promotion that year, and two, I might be passing up an opportunity that could, in fact, accelerate or ensure my promotion that year.

I carefully considered the position and thought about the risk of either possibility, and with my solid rationale in my back pocket, I decided to trust my instincts, take the risk, and accept the potential repercussions of turning it down, of saying no. The risk paid off. I was promoted that year and still maintained the support and sponsorship of my boss.

The person who can think out of the box, who will take the risk and test the normal way of doing things and is able to increase returns or garner extraordinary fees, for example, is an extremely valuable asset to any organization. Risk taking is like a muscle—in order for it to get stronger you have to work it out and exercise it. Typically, once you take a risk, you'll see that doing it wasn't so bad or as hard as you thought it would be. When I am about to try something new, I think about it, say a little prayer on it (because that's who I am) and then, like they say in the Nike commercial, I just do it. Unless you take risks, you won't stretch, you won't grow, and you won't gain. The way to get comfortable with taking risks is simply to take them.

It is important, especially early in your career, that you become comfortable with taking risks. As you get more and more senior, and more power and money is at stake, the competition gets stiffer and the evaluative measures—the platform for you to move ahead—become more subjective. You have to ask for the next promotion, pay raise, and new opportunity. Every time you ask, it is a risk, but surely you would agree that it is a risk worth taking. It is a part of the success equation, if you consider that success is moving ahead in an organization. If at the onset of your career you get in the habit of taking risks and articulating your expectations, as I talked about in Chapter Six, then you will be adept, skillful, and successful in taking on risks of more value as you move upward and onward.

CARLA'S PEARLS

- Success in a corporate environment involves stellar performance, integration into the politics, and risk taking. In today's highly competitive marketplace the "same ole, same ole" just won't do. If you're doing your job the way your predecessor was doing it, you, too, likely will soon find yourself a predecessor.

- There are two categories of risk: latent risks and forward risks. You cannot control, latent risks, but you can manage them by taking as many forward risks as possible.

- There are three types of risk: calculated risks, studied risks, and "step-out-on-faith" risks—take as many calculated risks as possible.

- The reason most people hesitate to take a risk is fear. But there is no downside to taking a risk. The worst that can happen is you'll fail. So what? Failure gives us the gift of experience. In the end more people regret not taking risks than taking them.

- No matter what your level of seniority or your position, you are an important part of the organization. Regardless of what level you are at, you shouldn't let your title dictate the risks you take.

- Just like saying yes to a new chance can be a risk, so can saying no. Have a solid rationale for turning down a new job or other opportunity and be willing to accept any potential repercussions and you'll likely be successful.

CHAPTER 8

POWER IN THE NETWORK
A Competitive Advantage

Relationships are one of the most important keys to success in any kind of business or career. Anyone who thinks they can achieve success on their own is in for a rude awakening. No one moves upward within an organization without the help and support of other people. You will need other people in your career advocating for you, clearing a path for you, using capital on your behalf (sponsors) in order for you to maximize your career success. Since many of the decisions that are made on behalf of your career are *not* based on merit, there will be times in your career when *who* you know will make the difference between getting or not getting the plum assignment, the great new job, the huge client, or the career-changing promotion.

Networking is one of the most commonly used terms in business. A network is nothing more than a series of connected relationships. Networks give you power. Your network is one of the most important competitive advantages you can have in business. When you graduate from college or graduate school, you have the name of your esteemed alma mater on your resume and it looks good. In addition, your grade point average and activities certainly are important to prospective employers. But *who* you know can often make the difference between you rather than one of your classmates getting the job.

If you are already settled in your career, *who* you know can make the difference between getting the promotion over one of your equally qualified colleagues. The bottom line? You need to know someone you can call, who will pick up the phone and make things happen on your behalf! You need to have relationships that are a part of a network.

In intensely competitive corporate environments, or even colleges and graduate schools, there are many outstanding, smart, and highly qualified candidates, and often no clear competitive differential among them. If one of the candidates has access to a relationship with a decision maker, that relationship will give them a distinct competitive advantage over other candidates, particularly if the skills and experience required are indistinct. Again, as we've talked about in previous chapters, it is human nature; we are all more comfortable with people we know than those we do not know.

Did you ever hear anyone say, "It's not what you know, it's who you know"? Well, truer words were never spoken. We live in a world where we are all connected and interdependent. You cannot be successful in today's corporate, academic, legal, medical, nonprofit, or other professional environment without being somehow reliant upon someone else. You are dependent on others for promotions, raises, new opportunities, or appointments. Even if you are an entrepreneur, you are dependent upon bankers or angel investors for financing for your business or people to get the word out regarding your goods and services; you are dependent upon customers to generate revenues. You need others to help you to accomplish your goals. Your source for these important relationships? Your network.

I challenge you to begin thinking of your network as a series of connected relationships. These relationships do not have to be literally connected to one another, but, rather, they should all be somehow connected to you. For you to find success in your career, you must learn to cultivate relationships—all kinds of relationships—with many different types of people. A common misstep many people make when building their network is only to reach out to people who look like them, are in the same age group, or are the same gender or ethnicity. That is a mistake. Like your "board of directors" that we discussed in the section on mentors (see Chapter 5), your network should be diverse ethnically, geographically, professionally, and with respect to gender, age, and extracurricular interests. You should think of your network as a source of leverage for your career, a source for learning, and a platform from which you can move throughout and upward in your career. While not everyone in your network necessarily will need to be a friend or even a fan, everyone in your network should have a role. Some people in your network may act as an information resource; they may offer you introductions to other important relationships or they may inform you about job openings or potential new assignments or projects.

My network is broad and wide. It includes not only investment bankers, lawyers, CEOs, CFOs, and consultants, but also teachers, heads of nonprofits, doctors, nurses, home health aids, recording artists, producers, actors, trainers, clergy, firemen, policemen, professional sports executives, and search consultants. It includes people who are senior to me, junior to me, and people who are at my level. It includes people who are close to me professionally, close personal friends, and still others whom I consider acquaintances.

People often ask me, "How do you know so many people? Why do so many people seem to know who you are?" The answer is that I make it my business wherever I go, whenever I have a new experience with new people, to strike up a conversation with someone I never met before and focus on who they are. At the same time, one of my goals is to make sure that by the end of our conversation they also have a good sense of who I am. I make a note of how I can stay connected to them. I firmly believe that you should *respect everyone*, no matter what their position, and *honor everyone's power* in life. We *all* have power, whether we recognize it or not. And as I approach every potential relationship, I think first of how I can be helpful to the other person instead of thinking of how they can help me. The reciprocity in the relationship usually comes over time. Remember, the way you treat your network is the way your network will treat you.

Your network gives you professional power; in fact, it *is* your power because it is a part of you. Your network is unique because you are unique; and the way *you* interact with people is very different than the way I, or someone else, would interact with the same people. You can have the same person in your network as someone else does, but your relationship with that person can be markedly different. That person may be willing to share information with you or introduce you to someone else in their network, but they might not be willing to do the same for someone else. You should honor the fact that your network is unique to you, particularly with respect to how its relationships function. You should be cognizant of this when making connections among the people who are in your network.

Your network should be a point of competitive advantage for you. The power in your network is not in the number of business cards you collect or the number of people that are in your network. The power of your network depends on the strength of your relationships, how well you manage the network, and your role within the network.

BUILDING A NETWORK

When establishing a network, think about what role you want to play. Do you want to be the connector—the person who matches up person A with person B over and over again? Do you want to be the information gatherer—the person who spreads information in the network both confidential and nonconfidential? Or do you want to be the helpful person—the person who leverages information and relationships on behalf of others?

I am often asked, "How do you build a network?" You can start building a network as early as high school. Your teachers, deans, principals, coaches, and even peers are all people who could be in your network. These people could be very helpful to you in your future endeavors. Teachers and deans write college and scholarship recommendations, they sing your praises (or not) in the community, and they can promote the brand that is *you* in the school community or the community at large. They influence what potential colleges consider you at the outset. College professors, tutors, and deans can influence the job you get after graduation and they can influence the graduate school you attend. They can also influence the job you get after graduate school or when you are moving from one firm to another early in your career, especially when you are just starting out and looking for that first big break or looking for that big promotion. While some companies might use executive search firms to look for candidates for a position, many times firms call deans of the various business schools, the headmaster of a particular institution, or even your classmates to find good candidates. That's how firms pick their shortlists of hires, and you want to be one of the few who make those shortlists by being at the top of your former dean's or professors' minds.

Your network is all the people you meet throughout your life who not only influence who you are as a person but who can influence your career's trajectory and direction. Almost any relationship that you have or seek to build has been, or could be, instrumental in your life. In building your network, first look at the relationships you currently have and think about how they have been helpful in influencing your career or personal life. Consider how they could be even more helpful if you leveraged them properly. Look at every relationship that you choose to nurture and any that you may shy away from, and ask yourself how and where these relationships can be useful in your life. Next, think of the relationships that might help you move forward in your career, target them, and seek to build or strengthen them. Ideally you will be able to use your existing network of relationships to help you to develop new ones.

Here is an example of how you can leverage your network to work for you. In 1999 when I decided to record and release my first CD, *Carla's First Christmas*, I didn't know a thing about how to record, where to record, how to find out about royalty arrangements, or how to find a producer, an engineer, or even a first-class studio to record in! I most certainly did not know anyone in the music industry who could help to market or distribute the finished product. While I bought as many books as I could on recording and promoting your own music, I accessed one of my internal professional relationships to help me get the ball rolling.

I took one of my colleagues, also an accomplished musician, out to lunch. I explained that I wanted to do a recording, market, and sell the record to raise money for two schools. During that lunch, he laid out the steps that I would have to take to acquire licenses to sing certain songs, and he told me I would need a producer, a strong engineer, good studio musicians, and the like. But most importantly, he agreed to introduce me to another colleague who had his own recording studio.

I then took that colleague out to lunch in the hopes that I could convince him to record my music, but instead he offered to introduce me to a friend of his who was the musical director of a Broadway show who might be willing to act as a producer. I later

auditioned for the Broadway musical director between his mati-
nee and evening performances and he agreed to help me produce
my first CD. This relationship helped me to find the right recording studio, engineer, mastering studio, manufacturer, and musicians, and was instrumental in creating, developing, and producing
my first commercial musical project.

Do you see the power in leveraging your network? One of my
financial services relationships led to an entertainment relationship that expanded my network and enabled me to produce something that established me as a recording artist. Further, the finished
product, the CD, has not only enabled me to do good things in
the community, but I've been able to use it as a differentiator, a
relationship builder and point of conversation with my financial
services clients. My singing skills did not create this product—
clearly they were a contributor—but it was leveraging the relationships that produced the desired outcome.

One of my senior internal sponsors had a close personal relationship with the CEO of a major music label and when it was
time to market and distribute the CD I again leveraged my network and asked him for an introduction to this person. He personally walked me over to meet the CEO and he agreed, in turn, to
introduce me to the president of their independent music distribution arm, which later agreed to distribute the record to all the
major retail chains. In addition, my firm gave me access to its press
relationships so I could properly generate interest in the CD's release. Another public relations relationship that I had formed as a
result of a deal I had worked on as a banker helped to get the attention of the *New York Times*, which printed a story about the CD in
the Sunday Business section in September 2000.

Your network is essential to everything that you do. As you
progress throughout your career, it is important to continue to
grow your network and nurture the key relationships within it.

Many people ask me how they can keep up with all of the relationships they have acquired in the limited time they have.

It is especially easy in today's environment to maintain your relationships by sending out periodic e-mails. Use e-mail to update your contacts on what's happening for you professionally and personally. Also let them know what your future goals are so that as they are approached with opportunities, your name is on their mind as a possible candidate. You should make it a point to have at least one face-to-face yearly interraction and at least four voice-to-voice interactions with your most important relationships: the rest of the updates can be done by e-mail. With relationships that are less relevant to your career agenda in terms of timing, you can maintain the relationships with an e-mail update once or twice a year.

TYPES OF RELATIONSHIPS

There are four key types of relationships that should be the foundation of your professional network: 1) upward relationships: people who are your superiors; 2) lateral relationships: people who are your peers and assistants to people who are senior to you; 3) downward relationships: people who are junior to you; and 4) external relationships: people who do not work within your firm, but who could be important to your work—people on non-profit boards or volunteer organizations you serve on or colleagues at other firms within and outside of your industry.

Upward relationships
It is essential to your professional success to have good relationships with people who are senior to you within the organization. These are the people in your environment who ultimately decide on your future within the organization. They determine

not only your pay, but also promotions, new assignments, projects, and other opportunities that could be essential to positioning you for the future. You should seek to not only have a relationship with your boss, but also with your boss's boss and even higher in the organization if possible, depending where you are in the hierarchy. As senior people become aware of who you are, you become a part of their thought process in terms of succession planning or deciding who to promote to a new opportunity. Your network of senior people can help to accelerate your visibility and the organization's knowledge of who you are.

To begin an upward relationship, think of ways of getting exposure to senior people. For example, some companies have periodic internal town halls and other meetings where the most senior people in the firm address employees about the state of the business, the competitive environment, the company's performance, and future plans. Make it your business to attend these meetings. Sit in the front row. Have a few well-thought-out questions prepared and deliver them in a precise, thoughtful, and articulate manner during the question and answer session that typically follows the meeting. After the meeting, go up and introduce yourself to the senior people. See if you can take the opportunity to have a quick one-on-one or arrange one for the future. Remember, you have one shot to make a good impression, so always be ready.

Afterward, think of what you have in common with the senior person that you can begin to build on for the next time you see them. Perhaps you went to the same undergraduate or graduate school. Perhaps the person is a sports buff and you have that in common. Maybe you both love to ski and you can talk about the various slopes you've visited, or maybe you both love golf and you can talk about the best courses. Look for other opportunities to get in front of the senior person at special group meetings or in recruiting forums. If there are volunteer projects or special task

forces that they support, get involved so you can gain the exposure that you need to further your relationship.

In the early days of my career, I did not always have access to
senior people. One of the things I found I liked to do was recruit
other people to the firm. I was passionate about my business and
I truly felt that my firm was one of the best, if not the best, on
Wall Street. I was quite effective at selling the firm to prospective
employees. After a candidate would receive an offer, the company
would bring them in for a "sell day." This was a day dedicated to
exposing potential candidates to different people within the investment banking division in an effort to heighten their enthusiasm to join the firm. This day always included several meetings
with the most senior people within the division. I quickly became
captain of a recruiting team early in my tenure at the firm, and
as such would often have to call senior people to enlist their help
in convincing the candidate to join the company. Making that
call and escorting the candidate to the various executive offices
gave me visibility with senior people throughout the division and
created a dialogue between us regarding the candidate. These
"recruiting" relationships became the foundation for future relationships when I later found myself working with one of those
senior people on a transaction, for example. It made transitioning
that relationship to my network much easier. After beginning those
relationships, I spent time trying to further them, finding ways to
interact with those senior people, even if it meant just swinging
by their office from time to time for a quick chat. The key was to
maintain contact so that I would further develop the relationship
and further establish it as part of my network.

The lateral network

Many types of people should be included in your lateral network. It should include your peers and the assistants to the senior

people who are important in your environment or who work for the senior people within your organization. If you have strong peer relationships at work, you will be perceived as someone who is integral to the organization, because it will be clear that your peers like and respect you. That goodwill will transcend to senior and even junior relationships.

It should also include peers who are at your level in other competitor organizations or in other industries that are directly related or tangentially related to your business. Your lateral network serves four important roles for you. It gives you: 1) access to relationships, 2) skills transfer, 3) information transfer, and 4) inspiration, camaraderie, or affirmation.

Your peer network

In some cases, your peers may have access to a better relationship with a senior person than you do. They may have attended the same undergraduate or graduate institution, grown up in the same town, or belong to the same secret society or country club as the senior person. You can use your peer networks to gain access to senior relationships by asking them to make introductions for you or including you in their social events. Once the introduction is made, it is up to you to nurture and grow the relationship. Remember that the relationships in your network, particularly your peer network, are reciprocal, and you should actively look for ways of assisting your peers with access to relationships or whatever else they might need.

Your peers may come to the organization with a different skill set than you have or they may catch on to a process or procedure before you do. If you have a strong relationship with your peers it will be easy to ask them to help you with or teach you something you need to know to be successful in your own endeavors.

Your peers can also help you understand the landscape of the organization. They may have exposure to certain people who, for example, are difficult to work for. They can give you tips on how to successfully navigate that. Do not be afraid to ask your peers for help because you fear showing your vulnerability. It is far more important that you get the help you need to excel in the environment than it is to preserve your pride. No one knows everything within any organization, and everyone needs help from time to time. Learn to get comfortable asking for help, because there will come a time when someone will be asking you. It is important that having a relationship with *you* is perceived as worthwhile in the eyes of your peer network. You want to be known as someone who is helpful in transferring skills, accessing relationships, and/or providing useful internal information.

If a number of other people join an organization at the same time as you do and they seem to fit into the company faster and better than you have, then it's likely due to their network and their ability to build relationships. It is time for you to target a couple of people you want to build relationships with to help you better integrate into the environment. It is often easiest to build these relationships outside of the office. Inside there may be political or other pressures that make building and solidifying that relationship a little more challenging.

When I first began my career as an associate, my incoming class of associates included a number of people who were former analysts at my firm, so they had a natural network. Of those people that were not former analysts themselves, their network included some of the former analysts; they had attended the same business school and formed and fostered those relationships there. These two groups were able to integrate into the organization much faster than I was able to because they had leveraged the former analyst network before and in the early days of our associate career. As such, they had relationships already established.

As I talked to various people about what was happening within the organization, I always felt that I was one of the last to hear the latest information or find out about certain people in the company. I knew that if I didn't do something soon, I would find myself at a political disadvantage because I did not have access to the information flow.

I sought out someone from my class who was *not* themselves a former analyst, but who had very strong relationships with some of the group. I also sought out a former analyst with whom I already had a budding relationship. I spent time fostering a relationship with each of them, often going out to lunch, dinner on the weekends, or for drinks after work. I asked for their help in gaining access to the information flow and I made my external network available to them as they requested. In a short period of time, I was being invited to more events with broader groups of people, and, as a result, I became a bigger part of my peer network. Over time, I began to get access to the same information flow as my peers because of the relationships that I had been introduced to through the two relationships I nurtured.

Another important benefit of your peer network is that it can offer you inspiration, camaraderie, affirmation, and support. Sometimes you can become distracted and discouraged when things are not going as you would like in your career. Your peer network, particularly your external peer network, can act as a source of comfort, affirming that you are not going through your circumstances alone, or that you are not the only person who has ever encountered a particular problem. Sometimes by sharing your issues with peers, you may find that not only have they been through the same thing, but they may have developed a solution or best practice for dealing with the problem.

Peers also can offer encouragement or advice to help advance you along the way. We typically don't want to share our issues or failures with our peers because we see them as competition. In an intensely competitive environment, I understand and agree that you want to be careful with whom you share information about yourself, but I would challenge you to change that thinking. There is plenty of room at the top. Not asking for help can not only hurt you, but worse yet, it can *keep you behind*. Sometimes the act of asking for help can be a foundation to building a terrific long-term peer relationship that can be very useful to you over time. While it's not necessarily the way we are conditioned to think, the truth is, you are *not* in competition with your peers. Instead, you are in competition with yourself. Don't shy away from a peer relationship because you think your peer is further along in their career or is moving ahead at a faster rate than you. Use your relationship to learn how you can move through the organization as fast as they seem to be moving. Whenever you feel like you want to move away from a relationship because you are intimidated or even envious of someone else, remember the phrase "Don't hate, gravitate." That's exactly the person you need to get closer to. Rather than be jealous, use your relationship with them to help you learn and grow.

We have a tendency to think we should know it all. The truth is, we can never be experts at everything and when we need help—and at some point we all will need help, it is important to have a strong network of colleagues to reach out to.

The assistant relationship

Another type of relationship vital to your professional network is your relationship with the assistants of those people who are senior to you. The assistants are the ultimate gatekeepers. I have seen so many people derail themselves by ignoring, or, worse yet, being rude to a senior person's assistant. They failed to recognize how important this person could be in their network of relationships. Remember what I said at the outset of this chapter? Everyone has power, and that power is to be honored in *everyone* in your network.

In most professional organizations, the person closest to the CEO, CFO, or COO is their assistant. Not only can the assistant get you access to the senior person, but they also can give you information on how intense their day was, what their mood might be, the best way to approach them, when to approach them, and so on. The assistant can set the context of your conversation, so that whatever you need to approach them with will be perceived in the best possible light. I cannot count the number of times I have needed access to an extraordinarily busy, senior person who in the normal course of business would have considered me to be low on their priority list. Normally I wouldn't be able to get an appointment for a very long time. But because I had fostered a good relationship with that person's assistant, I was squeezed in to see them, often on the very same day I requested a few minutes of their time.

How did I build some of my assistant relationships? By taking advantage of the opportunities that I had to interact with them; for example, when I was waiting outside of a senior person's office, at Christmas parties, in the cafeteria, or anyplace that I had an opportunity to chat with them. In most cases, they are women just like me, so we already have *a lot* in common to talk about. I also have been helpful on career day at their children's schools when they wanted a banker to come in and talk. I would make myself available to discuss colleges or music with their children, or if they needed help or a word of encouragement in their own professional development. You never know what you have to offer someone else and how that offer may be useful to you down the road as a part of the reciprocation in a relationship. When I offered myself to help them, I was not looking for something in return; it was the fact that I was *willing to be of service* in our relationship that it came back to benefit me later.

Downward relationships

The third key type of relationship in your network is the downward relationship. These are the people who are junior to you in age or rank. They are the people who are coming up behind you in your career. This is an important network to nurture, because these are the people that you potentially will lead now or in the future. You must understand them and they must respect you in order for you to do so. Your junior or downward relationships can be useful to you in three ways: 1) they give you insight into new trends; 2) they can teach you new skills; and 3) they may even provide you with access to other important relationships.

Recently I needed to meet someone in a senior government position to get useful information for a special project I was working on for my firm. One day over lunch, I happened to mention to one of my mentees, a young woman junior to me, that I needed access this to relationship. It turned out that *she* had a relationship with the very person I wanted to meet. She made a phone call for me and they immediately agreed to see me. I went on to have a very productive conversation with my new contact. I don't know how long it would have taken me to get access to this person, or if they ever would have agreed to see me, but by leveraging a junior person in my network, I was able to gain access to this important relationship.

Here's another great example: I was once asked to speak at a Fortune 500 company by a relatively junior colleague at another firm. She heard me speak at another venue and thought I would be a great addition to an event she was involved with. I agreed. After speaking to an audience of about three hundred people, I mentioned to her that I would like to have a personal audience with the

CEO of her firm, who had not been present at my speech. She immediately used her network with the CEO's assistant, and within a couple of days I was on the CEO's calendar. When I met with the CEO, we had a very good personal conversation, and I created an opportunity to follow up with business later. That one meeting led to a series of meetings and gave my organization access to a dialogue with the CEO and potential business in a way we previously had not had access to. This lateral/junior network relationship created leverage for me in my own organization and gave me access to an important senior upward relationship that I could add to my network and which ultimately benefited my organization.

In today's fast-paced, technologically driven world, many people in their late thirties, forties, and fifties are not as technologically advanced as many younger people in their late teens, twenties, and early thirties. However, it is the more seasoned professionals who are in power and who are the ones with the authority in organizations. Having junior people in your network will enable you to learn some of the technological and other newer skills that can help you to connect to the next generation of customers, employees, and shareholders; make you more efficient; and give you greater access to information. If you are a younger person in an organization, find ways of leveraging your technology and information skills for bridging to upward networks. If you are a more seasoned professional, use the junior network to gain access to those skills.

External networks

External relationships also are very important in your network, particularly if you are in a client-driven business such as financial services, sales, consulting, advertising, or law. It is important that you build your external network extensively. You never know who can introduce you to someone who might bring business to your firm.

I have the privilege of serving on several nonprofit boards for causes that are very important to me. As a result, I have not only had the opportunity to build relationships with corporate CEOs, but also with television personalities, music producers, civic leaders, and community leaders. Many have been monumental in furthering my professional agenda. Some of these external relationships also have positively influenced my internal relationships. They have articulated their positive interactions with me outside of the firm to my internal colleagues who may or may not have known me very well prior to hearing the good word about me.

The way to build your external networks is to consciously invest time and get involved. If you are working so hard that you only have time for your family and work, then you need to figure out how to restructure your days, weeks, and months to include time to build your other relationships. We already established that much of the power of who you are rests in who you know. Power is being able to make things happen or the ability to mobilize and influence others who can make things happen. You highlight and enhance your power in an organization when you have a relationship that the organization wants and needs to leverage. When you can leverage your network of contacts to make something happen, you can create significant value add for yourself in the company and further enhance your opportunity for success.

Your external network should include peers and senior people in competitor organizations, senior people in the industry that you are focusing on for your client referrals, entrepreneurs, medical professionals, civic leaders, and clergymen. You want to stay connected to what is going on in your industry and what competitors are doing. That information is value add in your organization. You want to have a network of people in the industry that you are focusing on for business so that you have an opportunity to build your pipeline. You want a network that includes entrepreneurs because they are not only a source of business but a potential professional opportunity should you ever want to go out and start your own venture. As we get older, understanding and navigating the health-care industry is essential, and having medical professionals in your network can be useful both personally and professionally. You might also want to include executive recruiters and headhunters in this group, as they have their finger on the pulse of what's happening in the industry in terms of compensation, bonuses, and job openings. Your relationships with civic leaders can be useful because every corporation is focused on maintaining its standing as a good corporate citizen. Relationships with government, community, and civic leaders will affect and influence that standing. I personally believe that strong relationships with clergy or other spiritual leaders are important to you personally because they help you to stay connected to the True Power Source.

There is power in your network, but you must recognize it, understand it, and use it. I have found that women in particular do not use their networks, and in many cases do not make themselves available and useful to their relationships within their network. Many women fail to realize that they have a network, a powerful series of connected relationships they can use to further their career. While men will quickly access their relationships and actively seek help to move forward, women tend not to use each other in that way. Failing to access and use your network is like failing to use your voice. You will create a competitive disadvantage for yourself because you are failing to use a source of power that is uniquely yours and that is a comparative and competitive differentiator for you.

Your network is one of the most important tools you can have to help further your career success. Properly using your network means respecting *every person's* power. Networking is not just about connecting with people who can do something for you. It is about building mutually beneficial relationships with various people at all levels within and outside of your firm. It is about openly and willingly offering your power for use on someone else's behalf.

- Relationships are one of the keys to success in any industry. Your network gives you power and is one of the most important competitive advantages you can have in business.

- Think of your network as a series of connected relationships. These relationships do not have to be literally connected to each other, but, rather, they are all somehow connected to you.

- Your network should be diverse and include all kinds of people, all ages, seniorities, and ethnicities, both genders, with varying interests. Everyone has power, and you should respect that power in each person regardless of their title or level of seniority.

- Your network should consist of at least four kinds of relationships: upward relationships with senior people; lateral relationships—those with your peers and the assistants of senior people in your network; downward relationships with people junior to you; and external relationships with people outside of your firm or industry, such as people on nonprofit boards that you serve on, at volunteer organizations, or colleagues at other firms both within and outside of your industry.

- Be willing to offer your assistance and also to receive it from others. Networking is a two-way street.

CHAPTER 9

BALANCE IS A NECESSITY
Use Your Passions to Achieve It

If I had to choose one area of focus that has helped me to stay motivated, to tolerate the volatilities of the market and the internal politics, stay interested in continuing to learn about and excel in my industry, and to realize all of the other accomplishments I have achieved as a professional, it would be that I have always sought to maintain balance in my life.

There is a lot of talk about work–life balance in corporate America today. Most people claim that it is impossible to obtain balance, particularly in highly competitive environments such as financial services. Many companies claim they want their employees to have that balance and put elaborate programs in place to promote it. But we all know the truth. When works gets crazy, when you've got endless deadlines and your boss is demanding you stay late once again, the first thing to suffer is your personal life, and anything that closely resembles balance goes right out of the window.

Many people define balance as managing their professional and their personal lives, particularly their family life. But I want to introduce a new definition of balance: integrating giving back and your passions into your professional life. I believe that in order to be truly successful at your job you need to have passions that contribute to your happiness, well-being, and who you are as a person. Balancing your work with your passions is a key to succeeding long term at anything in business, and in life! You must have something, whether it is activities or people, that you can rely on to make you feel good. You must have something that you are passionate about that makes you feel alive, that brings you joy to balance out the professional life that, no matter who you are or what your title, will *never* consistently fulfill you.

That's because professional life never goes smoothly *all* of the time—I don't care who you are. While our jobs are very important to us, your job cannot be *all* you have in your life. When your job is all you have, your life becomes a function of somebody else's day. If your job is all that's important to you, when your boss has a bad day, then you have a bad day. When the deal doesn't go well, then you'll have a bad week. If you get into a disagreement with a colleague on Friday, then your weekend is ruined. Do you see the pattern?

Whether it's your family, your significant other, working out at the gym, mountain climbing, going to church, running marathons, or taking cooking classes, you have to have something else that you are passionate about that gives you an opportunity to interact with others, feed yourself emotionally and spiritually, or lift someone else up. If it brings you joy, it should be a part of your daily life. That is the way to survive in organizations in which the stress level and demands on you are often very high. Don't get so caught up in a job that you don't do something every day that makes you feel alive and happy. That's how you continue to refuel.

The most common reason that people use for not having balance is that they don't have time for _____ (fill in the blank) outside of work. I have heard countless people say that after a fourteen-hour day, there are a couple of hours left for family, and nothing else. I don't buy it. If there is something that any of us really wants to do, we find a way to make it happen. My strategy: Calendarize it.

First map out a typical day. Look at places where you lose time, where you are not as productive as you would like to be, and capture time there. Look at what you do with your lunch break; most of us have at least five hours or as many as ten hours a week for lunch. Do you have to have lunch with internal or external clients every day? What happens if you take two hours a week during your lunch break to do something that brings you joy? If it's art, take lunch at a museum; if you are into fitness, use the time for a workout; if you like to perform, take a singing lesson at lunch; or check out a noontime lecture or church service. If you want more time with your kids, visit their day-care center or school and have lunch with your child and some of their friends. There are countless things you can do with just one hour.

Another trick that I use to create more time is to congregate like actions together and challenge myself to finish by a certain time. How many times have you tried to read a memo or a piece of research and then find yourself distracted by answering an e-mail, talking to someone who stops by, or answering a phone call? Suddenly you find it takes you twice as long to get it done. When I know that I have several things to read and absorb, I group those things together and focus on nothing but that for an hour or two. I hold all calls or interruptions for that period until I am done. I do the same thing for e-mails. Instead of trying to answer e-mails throughout the day, I pick several half-hour slots during the day when I do nothing but answer e-mails. I have picked up several hours of time in my day using this congregate strategy, and this has created more time. And by having more time and the opportunity to integrate some of the things that I am passionate about into my day, I also find that I am further motivated to give my attention to greater performance in my professional job.

Community service is one of my greatest personal passions. Not only does giving back help others, but I have found being of service has been a significant contributor to propelling my professional career. I certainly am not suggesting that you give to get something in return, not at all. For me, the giving itself has been its own reward. I truly enjoy helping people. No matter how demanding my schedule becomes, I still maintain time to be of service to other people. It is part of my success equation, and because of this I can always find energy to expend in this department. I have been fortunate in my life and career, and I am so grateful for all that I have. One of the ways I balance out the many intense hours that I expend as a banker and say thank you for all of the gifts that I have received is to use all of the intellectual, experiential, and financial assets that I have obtained to help others.

Many of us enjoy jobs that offer good salaries, benefits, and other perks that make our lives very comfortable. I believe giving back is something we have to do simply because of who we are, that we have a responsibility to give back. It's a way to say thank you for all of our blessings, to make a positive contribution to the world around us; it makes us feel good, it takes the focus off of our day-to-day business concerns and puts it on those people who are not as fortunate as we are. It reinforces why we are working so hard, why moving up the corporate ladder is so important, and it underscores the widespread impact we can have on the lives of other people.

In my opinion, the secret is that when you give back, you also multiply your own blessings and your own success. I serve on nonprofit boards for organizations and causes I believe in. And as a result I have met potential clients and prospects. You never know who may be sitting in the chair next to you at that nonprofit board meeting, at the school where you are painting the gymnasium, in the community where you are sprucing up the park, or whose mother or father you are visiting at the nursing home.

As you already know, one of my other passions is singing, gospel singing in particular. I perform around the country at various events and churches and sing with my church choir, the St. Charles Gospelites. I found a way to marry my passion for gospel singing with community involvement by giving the proceeds from my CDs and performing concerts for which the proceeds are distributed to two schools, St. Charles Borromeo School in Harlem and Bishop Kenny High School in Jacksonville, Florida. Not only has it been extremely rewarding for me personally; it also has helped me in business in many unexpected ways.

Personally, it goes without saying how great it feels to be able to contribute all the proceeds from my Carnegie Hall concerts and the CDs I've recorded (I'm currently working on my third), but it also had a surprising result for me professionally. Here is one example: As a banker, you live and breathe to get your name or a quote in the business section of the *New York Times*, the *Wall Street Journal*, or the *Financial Times*. It is something all bankers strive for, whether we admit it or not. There's an unspoken understanding that a mention or a quote in either paper affords you a certain level of professional respect.

By 2000, after twelve years as a banker, I had never been mentioned in either publication, so you can imagine how happy I was when on September 22, 2000, after just releasing my first CD, *Carla's First Christmas,* that a reporter wrote an article titled, "Manager Sings of a Manger!" Think about how all the components of my life came together by making a recording CD, something I love to do. My faith is extremely important to me and is another one of my personal passions: I recorded a CD in God's name about the birthday of his son, Jesus, and every dime of the proceeds from the concerts and CD sales went to the schools. I end up with an article, not just in the Business section of the *New York Times* but in the Sunday *New York Times*, the most prestigious business section of any newspaper in the country.

Now, do I need to ask you how much my stock with clients and internally at Morgan Stanley went up by Monday morning? People were passing me in the hallway saying, "Hey, Carla, saw you in the *New York Times*—good job." "Great article, Carla." Many of these people had never even looked my way before! Then in February 2006 an article titled, "An Investment Banker's Credo: Good Business, Good Music, Good Works" appeared in the *Wall Street Journal*, written by Ashley Khan; it was a half-page story on my first Carnegie Hall concert, which was a sold-out show. Interestingly enough, the writer chose to focus on my show rather than all the challenges Morgan Stanley was going through at the time, or any of the deals that I'd worked on. Instead, the journalist wrote about gospel music and what I was trying to do with my music in spreading the Word and helping the schools.

After that article appeared, I received countless calls from clients thanking me for having the courage to talk about my faith so openly. "I never thought I'd see a banker do that," said one of my clients. "Now I feel like I can close my door and get on my knees when I need to. Thank you very much for freeing me." This call and others like it came from clients who, before reading the article, didn't even know that I had a church affiliation. Nor did I know that any of them would identify with it. It was an interesting and very important lesson for me. Simply by being myself and honoring my passion for helping others, my career relationships expanded even further and in ways I never imagined. Seeking to have balance in my life and making an important place for my personal passions and interests not only gave me satisfaction; it also brought notice to me in my career as well. It was a win-win for me.

Oh, and by the way, for a singer, standing on the stage and performing at Carnegie Hall? Priceless!

Participating in community service has helped me build relationships with my clients as well. I've lost track of how many times when I'm trying to get to know a new client, working on building a relationship, during a conversation the topic of community service comes up. They are often doing some interesting and amazing volunteer work with an organization they feel passionate about, and, in turn, they want to hear about what I am working on. It not only becomes an opportunity to engage in good, positive conversation, it's a great common point of interest for us both.

Personally, giving back refuels me over and over. It not only allows me to balance my personal and professional life; it is personally rewarding. It feels good to help other people: there is no other feeling like it in the world.

If you are in financial services or any kind of service business, your clients are likely doing the same thing with their free time. So talk about what you're doing with United Way, in your church, or with the Girl Scouts. It not only makes you feel good, which we all need more of, it contributes something positive to the world, and can also be an important bridge to building a professional relationship. And as I talked about in Chapters 2, 5, and 7, relationships are key elements of your career success. And who knows what might happen for you?

Giving is not only the right thing to do for me. It also keeps me humble and reminds me that there is another world outside of Wall Street where my gifts, talents, and abilities can be useful, and it provides meaning and balance in my life. It is my passion. It helps me to maintain balance. What is your passion? How can you get more of it into your day?

CARLA'S PEARLS

- In order to be truly successful at your job and in your life, you must have balance: Integrate giving back with your passions in your professional life. It is critical to have passions that contribute to your happiness, well-being, and who you are as a person.

- While our jobs are very important to us, your job cannot be *all* you have in your life. When your job is all you have, your life becomes a function of somebody else's day.

- If it brings you joy, it should be a part of your daily life. Whether it's your family, your significant other, working out at the gym, mountain climbing, going to church, running marathons, or taking cooking classes, you have to have something that you are passionate about that gives you an opportunity to interact with others, feed yourself emotionally and spiritually, or lift someone else up.

- The secret is that in giving back, you also multiply your own blessing and your own success. Being yourself and honoring your passions will not only give you personal satisfaction; it will also expand your career. It's a win-win proposition.

- Giving back is a constant reminder that there is another world outside of our jobs where our gifts, talents, and abilities can be useful to ourselves and others.

CHAPTER 10

EXPECT TO WIN
Show Up with Your Best Self Every Day

I have always believed that if you approach your career expecting to succeed, you will. When I get up in the morning, I start out with the intention that I am going to be triumphant in my day. It is a decision I make every morning. This decision is supported by my spiritual belief and my number-one mantra: "I can do *all* things through Christ who strengthens me" (Philippians 4:16). I think about what I have to accomplish that day and look forward to the tasks I have at hand. I believe that every experience, good or bad, every class, every deal, has already given me the skills or judgment that I need to do a stellar job. And if you want to succeed you have to do the same. You have to walk into your office each day expecting to win. Your power to execute lies in your expectation, that you will have the ability to perform exceedingly well in whatever project, assignment, or routine task that lies ahead of you.

Midway through my career I found myself in the midst of a really tough year. I had worked on deals that didn't go well. For a couple of years I didn't get paid what I had wanted to be paid. As a result of those experiences, I found myself becoming less and less sure that I would achieve all of my goals. I began to think that maybe I wouldn't get the promotions I wanted or have the successful career I had planned. I started questioning myself, my abilities, and my decisions. My confidence was very low.

Tired of feeling down and discouraged, I knew I couldn't continue on that way. I had to do something to change things. I started to think back to a time when I had more belief in myself. I wondered, "What's the difference between Carla at eighteen and Carla at thirty-something?" I realized that Carla at eighteen always *expected* that she would win. Call it wide-eyed optimism or the blissful ignorance of youth if you will. But I always knew that I would go to a great undergraduate institution, and I did—I went to Harvard. I always expected I'd get into the law school or the business school of my choice, and I did—I went to Harvard Business School. I always anticipated that I'd go to work for a great Wall Street firm, and here I am at Morgan Stanley. It never occurred to me that what I wanted might not happen.

So what happened to change that? I guess by the age of thirty-something a little of life had happened to me. Things didn't work out exactly as I had expected, I had a few unexpected challenges, and I started to think that maybe I wasn't as good as I thought. Perhaps I wasn't really cut out for this career long term. I began to think that maybe I couldn't rectify the perceptions that had been created by the mistakes I made. I allowed myself to get distracted by those mistakes and did not focus on the truth: that I had the intelligence, training, and ability to do a very stellar job as an associate, vice president, and beyond. I had the ability to turn around the current trajectory and reemerge on the road to success. These are the truths that I started to focus on. Rather than starting the day with positive expectations, I was approaching the day worried that I would make another mistake and further substantiate the perceptions that may have been created from my mistakes. I worried that my peers and superiors did not think highly of me, or that I wouldn't get promoted, and I was afraid that I wouldn't be paid what I believed I deserved. If you approach your day in this way—stressed, lacking confidence in yourself and your abilities, you are opening the door to failure and poor performance at every turn. You will attract the very experience or person that you fear.

As a woman of faith, I truly believe in the passage from Proverbs 23: "For as he thinketh in his heart, so is he" (KJV). When I was eighteen years old, it never occurred to me that I wouldn't be successful at whatever I wanted to do. But as a few things went wrong, my internal language, the things I thought and said to myself, started to change. Rather than *know* I could achieve all I wanted, I started to think that *maybe* I would be successful; I started to *hope* things would work out. These were mediocre thoughts, and I was getting mediocre results in my career.

You have to tell yourself every day that you *know* what you want to achieve will happen. And if you don't truly believe it, you have to, as the kids say, act "as if." When you are in an intensely competitive environment, people cannot only smell doubt on you; they can particularly smell fear, and they will try to take advantage of it. Plus, when you project a lack of confidence, when choosing people for the best assignments or projects, others won't necessarily think of you first. If you go around thinking, "*Maybe* I am good enough, smart enough, and capable enough to succeed," they'll think, "*Maybe* we should choose Adrienne, or maybe we should choose someone else." You have to work to get yourself to a place to *know* for sure that you're the right person for the job. If you don't believe in yourself, then why *should* anyone else? You can be sure no one else will either. You have to have a winner's expectations.

THE WINNER'S LENS

In order to maintain a winner's expectation you have to be able to see yourself through the lens of a winner. You must think like a winner, by following these five principles:

1. A winner always understands that they will achieve the best outcome. They identify very early on what the *best* outcome is and devise a strategy of how to get there.

2. A winner has a measure of fearlessness. They are never afraid to take on a challenge and are always confident that the outcome will be a good one for them: either they will accomplish their intended goal or they will learn a very valuable lesson that will be useful to them in the future. No matter what the outcome, they know they will get something extremely valuable from the experience. My winning fearlessness comes from the support of Romans 8:28 "All things work together for the good to them that love God, to them who are called according to His purpose."

3. A winner has the attitude that everything they endeavor to do will work out for their good. A winner never fears the outcome.

4. A winner understands that they cannot achieve their goals on their own. They understand that there is no I in TEAM and that they need to recognize and participate in interdependent relationships in order to move ahead.

5. A winner seeks to acquire the necessary skills to accomplish their goals. They do not rely on luck or political acumen to move forward. They seek to become the *best* in their area of expertise. A winner does not simply seek to be one of the pack; they always seek to be the positive outlier.

If you have a solid strategy for accomplishing your goals, you act with fearlessness, you respect and create interdependent relationships, and you focus on getting the skills and experiences that will give you credibility, you will have the foundation for a winning, expectant attitude and you will attract success.

When I was feeling *maybe,* about myself, I went back to my agenda and reminded myself of my original goals and purpose for coming to Morgan Stanley in the first place. I was on a business trip alone in my hotel room in Cleveland. It was the night before my birthday and I decided I wanted my next year to be different; rather than mediocre, I wanted the following year to be something very special. So I took some time to sit down and reflect on the previous twelve months.

I had first gone through this process when I was just thirteen years old and moving up from eighth grade to high school. I had decided I wanted to be a different person in high school. In junior high I was always in the mix, so to speak; I spent a lot of time talking about people, gossiping with the crowd. I knew everybody's business. But I decided I didn't need to know who was dating who, or what they had done on Saturday night. It was no longer important for me to know all of the latest gossip. I didn't want to be that person anymore; I wanted to be different. I wanted to spend my time focusing on me, my life, and who I wanted to be. I set that intention back when I was just thirteen years old, and that is still who I am today. I am a good friend. If you tell me something, it stays with me. My friends all know they shouldn't ask me anything about what one of our other friends is doing, because they know good and well they won't get any gossip from me.

As an adult, nearly twenty years later sitting alone in that hotel room, I was attempting to do the same thing. I wasn't making resolutions; it was really an exercise in self-reflection. I was conducting a personal assessment of who I had been in the past year and who I wanted to be in the next one. I wrote things such as, "I am a good friend, trustworthy, accessible; you can always find Carla if you need her." In terms of my job, I wrote, "I want to be known in the industry, as a professional and an expert at my craft." What this exercise did was give me guidance on how to conduct myself both personally and professionally.

I recommend doing this to everyone, especially if you feel that you might not have a strong enough sense of who you are or who you want to be. Set aside some time to sit down and think. All you need is four pieces of paper and a pen. At the top of each sheet of paper write:

Who have I been this year?
Who do I want to be?
What lessons have I learned this year?
What do I want to accomplish in the next year?

If you have trouble doing this exercise, try approaching it in the abstract, as if you were writing about someone else. Sometimes it's easier to describe others than it is to describe ourselves. Under "Who have I been this year?" you would write, "Terry has been a conscientious, hard-working employee, she always goes the extra step, and she is generous with her time, smart, and always has a good attitude." Under "Who do I want to be?" you might write, "Hope is always upbeat, working to contribute more creative ideas, and is a risk taker," and so on. In order for this process to be useful, your list has to include not only your strong points; it also should include any weaknesses, things you need to work on and improve.

As a result of doing this exercise I began to say no to those negative thoughts. As I looked at the lists of all of my good qualities and accomplishments, I remembered that I had the power. I had the choice to either focus on the negatives, the money I hadn't made, or the deals I wasn't getting, or I could decide to look at all of the good things about me, consider my agenda, and then develop a plan to turn the situation around and focus on how and when I was going to do that.

After all, I was *choosing* to walk in the front door of Morgan Stanley every day. I didn't have to. I could make a different choice. I had to stop throwing away my power by focusing on what was wrong and focus on ways, to use a baseball term, "to knock the cover off the ball." In other words, I had to decide that I was going to take pride in what I had accomplished and focus on doing well going forward, doing better every day so that when the next opportunity rolled around I would be ready.

Whatever you do, you have to approach it expecting that you are going to be successful. Every client you meet, every presentation you give, every business plan you write should be approached with a belief in yourself, knowing that you have all the tools necessary to do well.

When I was on the syndicate desk, I often would not meet the CEO and CFO of the company we were executing a deal for until we were about to go on the road to meet the investors. I knew that I had about two hours to talk with them and start to build a relationship before the road show began and we started to market the transaction.

Even though I literally had just met them, I knew I was going to be the one who was going to execute and price their very important deal for them over a span of about ten days! No matter what the circumstances, I had to go into the situation believing that everything would go well and that I would find a way to have them trust me and my advice for the next couple of weeks. When I walked in to meet them, I expected things to go well; I anticipated that they would have a favorable impression of me and that we could build from there. In almost every case, it worked!

Expecting to win, my body language changed, my speech changed, and my mentality changed. Everything about me reflected a winner's attitude. This even works when things don't go so well, and sometimes they don't—that's a fact of life. When things don't work out as I hoped, I try to view the experience as an opportunity for an unexpected valuable lesson.

One of the best ways to stay motivated is to give your all every single day. I bring all of Carla Harris to the table every day. I believe God gives his best to me every day, and as a result I feel it is my responsibility to myself, the people around me, and to Him to do the same. When I am feeling low because of what somebody did or said to me, or about something that's happened, or some of my plans aren't working out or have gone wrong, I simply stop and ask myself, "What can you do today, Carla, for somebody else, to lift them up? What are the things under your control that you can do to move someone else and, therefore yourself, forward?"

When I start to do those things, whatever it is—making the call, sending the e-mail, arranging the meeting, doing the research—my posture changes, my attitude is positive, and eventually as the day goes on, I start to feel better, I reclaim my power and get myself back on track. That is the mark of a successful person. Focus on what you *can* control, put one foot in front of the other, and keep on walking. That's how you keep yourself motivated.

If you find yourself feeling complacent or stagnant, go back to your agenda (see Chapter 2). This is your everyday guide. It reminds you why you took the job, why you wanted to work for the firm in the first place and what experience you wanted to get. Review the items on your agenda and ask yourself whether you are getting the experiences, meeting the people you wanted to meet, and living the lifestyle you envisioned. If the answer is yes, then you just need to think about those things you can control. But if the answer is no, then perhaps your agenda needs adjustment; it may just be time for a new set of goals. And you need to look for ways to meet those goals either inside or outside of the firm.

In financial services, for example, it's really hard to get bored. It's always changing. Interest rates get cut a percentage point, there's a sub-prime mortgage debacle, the Fed has a meeting and one of the governors says something at lunch that upsets the entire market and sends it plunging, a big firm goes bankrupt, the markets soars 300 points in one day and then plunges 250 the next. Every day is different, as is every deal, every company you work with, every strategy attached to every deal, and every context in which you are doing the deal.

There is no industry set up with a crystal ball to predict what the day will bring. But you can be sure, that no matter what your job, the day will bring something new. Life is about change. It is one of the few guarantees in life—change is inevitable, no matter how many plans you've made. If you approach your day looking forward to the changes and opportunities it brings, you are less likely to become complacent.

PART OF HAVING A WINNER'S ATTITUDE IS BEING COMBFORTABLE WITH AND WELCOMING CHANGE. IF YOU CAN CREATE CHANGE? EVEN BETTER!

On the other hand, if you feel you have mastered what you're doing and can knock the cover off the ball without trying, then that's a different issue. When you get to the point where you are no longer challenged by what you do and it has become rote, then it may be time to either look to do something else or work someplace else.

The reason is because if you are bored and not challenged in most careers, it's hard to stay sharp and motivated. In that state you won't perform in the way you need to in order to remain relevant. You don't ever want to get too comfortable. If you are sleep-walking through your day, you simply won't be as effective.

Successful people never become complacent. That's why they are always able to stay ahead of both the current and emerging competition. Successful people always maintain the attitude of trying to be the best. They keep up with the competition by keeping abreast of what's happening and coming up with fresh ideas, new products, marketing strategies, and processes. All of this married with their years of experience sets them apart and above the competition every time.

Winners are flexible with their careers and never attached to specifics. Be careful not to ignore wins, blessings, and opportunities because they don't appear looking like you thought they would. While I certainly have had definite expectations about what I wanted out of my career, I have also learned over the years not to be wedded to specifics.

Promotions sometimes come at a different time than anticipated. New opportunities have been offered to me unexpectedly. Dealing with unexpected changes in the script is what winners do, and they always have an expectation that the unanticipated surprise will hold a benefit or advantage for them.

The most important thing, as I discussed in Chapter 1, is to know who you are. No matter what situation, what circumstance, what job you are offered, if you don't know who you are, you are going to be easily and constantly distracted—distracted by organizational changes, by mergers and buyouts, and by other people's moods or agendas. You are going to find yourself overly obsessed with failures and overly sensitive to criticism. You can't be what I call selectively motivated, where you can only work hard and smart when things are going well. Learn who you are, focus on your agenda, and not only you, but the people you work with and everyone around you, will win. Knowing who you are allows you to present and sell yourself and your abilities in any situation, whether it's a good market or a challenging one.

People often ask me, "Carla, when will you stop? How will you know when you've achieved all that you can achieve?" Honestly, I don't think that my drive to succeed or my expectation to win will ever leave me. I think I'll really feel successful when I can look anyone in the eye and say, "You can do it" to whatever it is they want to achieve, and they'll believe me based on who I am and what I have achieved. We all need that kind of support sometimes. When I can offer that to people, when I have that credibility, then I will know I have done my job.

Even when I retire, I plan to keep striving and achieving. I'll work on my golf game and continue trying to find ways to perfect it. I'll look to do more with some of the nonprofits that I'm interested in. No matter what stage you are at in your career, you must look at your job, at your life, through the lens of a winner. Challenge yourself every day to be creative and masterful. And believe that you are capable and powerful. Every experience you have, good or bad, makes you a smarter and richer person. Having a winner's mentality makes the difference on day one of your career as well as in the last day of year thirty. Expect to win and you will.

CARLA'S PEARLS

- Approach each day believing that you will be triumphant and successful.

- Your thoughts influence your success—mediocre thoughts produce mediocre results—so *know* that you will win.

- Spend time in self-reflection. Decide who you want to be, and assess your successes and failures. Have goals to accomplish in the year ahead. Allow your lists to guide your life and refer to them when you need to in order to stay on track.

- To stay motivated, bring all of yourself to the table every day. Stay ahead of the competition by keeping abreast of what's happening, coming up with fresh ideas; use this with your experience to set yourself apart.

- No matter what stage you are at in your career, you must look at your job, at your life, through the lens of a winner. Challenge yourself every day to be creative and masterful. Expect to win and you will!

CHAPTER 11

MY MOST PRECIOUS PEARL

The pearl of authenticity, the pearl of setting your own agenda, the pearl of risk taking, the pearl of leveraging your voice, and the rest of the pearls in this book have all been instrumental in helping me to achieve success in my career, and I am confident that they will be useful to you, too, no matter what industry you work in.

One of the most important pearls, however, and the one that has been and continues to be the most powerful, is the pearl of understanding not only who I am, but *whose* I am. It's the eleventh pearl: I am a child of God. Understanding what who I really am means, and how it empowers me in my life, is the key reason that I have been able to weather the intense, tumultuous storms of volatility and challenges that exist in every industry, but certainly more acutely in financial services in general, and investment banking in particular.

As I said in Chapter 1, you have to bring your best self, your authentic self, to work every day. So I would not be giving you the true and authentic Carla in this book if I did not share how I have relied and depended upon and actively used my faith and spirituality as a tool for my success on Wall Street. My faith in God and my belief in His Word has carried me through tough times in my career: times when I was trying to make tough decisions about whether I should continue in the same job or continue working with the same product or at the same firm; times when I was learning to understand and navigate choppy political waters, trying to discern the supporters from the detractors; and times when I had to make a critical deal judgment where the answer was unclear, but where one decision yielded a very successful outcome and the other could have resulted in catastrophe. Time and time again, I have emerged successfully from crises, tough decisions, learning experiences, and tricky judgments because of the grace of God. I believe the Spirit that dwells within me powers the confidence and winner's attitude that I spoke of in Chapter 10 with the tenth pearl: Expect to Win.

My journey to owning and harnessing my spirituality was born out of a few tough, unfamiliar experiences. These experiences tested my record of achievements and tested my belief that I was in control of my life, my future, and the outcome of anything that I endeavored to accomplish. While I grew up in the church and was baptized at three months old, I didn't really begin paying attention to the power of prayer and focusing on God until I began my career and a few things weren't going the way I thought they should.

It was only then that I started to realize that perhaps I was not, as I thought, in complete control of what was happening in my life. Certainly I could work hard, make sure I stayed on top of the new industry products and trends, and insert myself into the politics of the organization. Yet I still found that I did not get the plum assignments that *I* wanted, I did not get the promotions *when* I thought that it was time to get one, or I did not get the platform that *I felt* I deserved. Those experiences taught me that there could, and would, be situations and timing I could not control: The political power brokers in an organization change overnight, your sponsor leaves abruptly, or someone makes a decision to give a colleague an assignment that you deserve; these are irreparable decisions, and there is nothing you can do to change them. Or someone in your family gets seriously ill or you get sick and you have to take a step back in your career just when things were on a roll. I learned that no matter how hard I prepared, no matter how much I did all of the things that I was supposed to do, that things could turn out differently from how I had planned.

This is when I started to realize that if I wanted to be able to "manage through" the things that I couldn't control, then I needed to have faith that the outcomes, even the surprise outcomes or particularly hard or difficult outcomes, would be in my favor. If I couldn't believe that, then how would I manage through a major disappointment? If I didn't believe that in the end everything worked out in my life the way God intended, then how could I have the energy, discipline, and tenacity to forge ahead, no matter what the outlook appeared to be?

It became clear to me that I couldn't make it alone, that my faith needed to be placed squarely in God. I began to understand that I had two choices: Either I could choose to trust Him, or I could choose to question and doubt Him and try to do things my way. I chose to trust Him, and thus began my desire and then my understanding of how to integrate my spirituality with my professional self.

It was during these times that I started to really pay attention to the prayers that I routinely said, such as the Lord's Prayer that begins, "Our Father who art in heaven, hallowed be thy name, thy kingdom come, thy will be done" and the 23rd Psalm, which starts, "The Lord is my shepherd; I shall not want." I started to understand what these prayers really meant. I started to spend more time really reading the Bible and comprehending the promises made to me, the birthrights given to me as a child of God. I started to pay careful attention to the messages as I never had before.

During my second year as an associate, I was having a really tough time in my career. I was working for someone who was very insecure and not really capable of or interested in training me. One afternoon, I was sharing my job worries with the mother of one of my dearest friends. She said, "Carla, read and pray Psalm 91, the Psalm of Protection, and Psalm 4."

1. *He that dwelleth in the secret place of the most High shall abide under the shadow of the Almighty.*

2. *I will say of the Lord, He is my refuge and my fortress: my God; in him will I trust.*
   —PSALM 91 (KJV)

1. *Hear me when I call, O God of my righteousness: thou hast enlarged me when I was in distress; have mercy upon me, and hear my prayer.*
   —PSALM 4 (KJV)

These two psalms became my daily mantra, my spiritual armor, and then, eventually, my comfort, my inspiration, and my motor to power through any professional challenge.

As I matured in my spiritual walk, I started to realize that I could use my faith as a tool for success. I viewed my faith as the steady constant against the backdrop of volatility and uncertainty that exist in the financial markets and in almost every industry that I can think of. I started to realize that no matter what happened in my career, I would have to consider it all good. I began to see everything that happened in my life as either a lesson or a blessing; each were valuable and were to be used and leveraged to keep moving forward and upward.

I also realized that because God gives me His best every day, then my job was to give my best in all of my endeavors. Further, if for some reason I found that I could not give my best, then I needed to find out why. If I wasn't being challenged, motivated, treated fairly, or whatever the issue, then it was *my* job to identify the problem, use my tools (my intelligence, experience, faith, and, of course, the pearls) to find the solution and then faithfully give the rest over to Him.

As my spiritual walk continued to develop, I spent even more time reading the Bible and getting into the Word. I began to develop an understanding of how some of the principles could, and should, influence and affect my daily life. I started to connect the dots between the Word and how it applied to me as a professional. In fact, I found several scriptures that really started to influence my outlook and I would use them to regain focus, especially when I became distracted by the stress of the job or the busyness of the business, or I experienced a few deals that went bad. I started to identify with the confidence that comes along with certain scriptures and began to apply them to whatever challenge emerged or to use them as daily motivation:

I can do all things through Christ which strengtheneth me.
PHILIPPIANS 4:13 (KJV)

=

No challenge at work is insurmountable.

Be careful (anxious) for nothing
PHILIPPIANS 4:6–8

=

Don't worry about anything.

No weapon that is formed against thee shall prosper
Isaiah 54:17 (KJV)

=

**Those who might wish me ill or try to derail me
from my agenda, WILL NOT prevail.**

*The will of God will not lead me where the Grace of God
won't protect me*

=

**Even though I may be in uncharted waters,
I will get what I need to be successful.**

*. . . all things work together for good to them that love God,
to them who are the called according to his purpose.*
Romans 8:28 (KJV)

=

**Even though things may not look good,
they will all work out for my benefit.**

*Fear thou not; for I am with thee: be not dismayed; for I am
thy God: I will strengthen thee; yea, I will help thee; yea, I will
uphold thee with the right hand of my righteousness.*
Isaiah 41:10 (KJV)

=

**No person or situation has been created that
I should fear. With God, I cannot lose.**

I will never leave thee, nor forsake thee.
Hebrews 13:5 (KJV)

=

**He is with me through all things. I need not fight
any battles on my own.**

I have never made a professional judgment without calling on the wisdom of the Spirit of God. That's what I believe in, and that belief sustains me in and through my life.

No matter what you believe in, you need something to turn to, something to call on for support and strength during those difficult and challenging times in our lives that we all face. You must have something in your life over and above your job that you can turn to for strength and guidance and comfort. You need a strong platform from which to build your success.

• • •

After this manner therefore pray ye: Our Father which
art in heaven, Hallowed be thy name.
Thy kingdom come, Thy will be done in earth, as it is in heaven.
Give us this day our daily bread.
And forgive us our debts, as we forgive our debtors.

And lead us not into temptation, but deliver us from evil:
For thine is the kingdom, and the power,
and the glory, for ever. Amen.
The Lord's Prayer, MATTHEW 6:9-13 (KJV)

• • •

The LORD is my shepherd; I shall not want.
He maketh me to lie down in green pastures:
he leadeth me beside the still waters.
He restoreth my soul: he leadeth me in the paths of
righteousness for his name's sake.
Yea, though I walk through the valley of the shadow of death,
I will fear no evil: for thou art with me; thy rod and thy staff they
comfort me.

Thou preparest a table before me in the presence of mine enemies: thou anointest my head with oil; my cup runneth over.
Surely goodness and mercy shall follow me all the days of my life: and I will dwell in the house of the LORD for ever.
Psalm 23 (KJV)

• • •

He that dwelleth in the secret place of the most High shall abide under the shadow of the Almighty.

I will say of the LORD, He is my refuge and my fortress: my God; in him will I trust.

Surely he shall deliver thee from the snare of the fowler, and from the noisome pestilence.

He shall cover thee with his feathers, and under his wings shalt thou trust: his truth shall be thy shield and buckler.

Thou shalt not be afraid for the terror by night; nor for the arrow that flieth by day;

Nor for the pestilence that walketh in darkness; nor for the destruction that wasteth at noonday.

A thousand shall fall at thy side, and ten thousand at thy right hand; but it shall not come nigh thee.

Only with thine eyes shalt thou behold and see the reward of the wicked.

Because thou hast made the LORD, which is my refuge, even the most High, thy habitation;

There shall no evil befall thee, neither shall any plague come nigh thy dwelling.

For he shall give his angels charge over thee, to keep thee in all thy ways.

They shall bear thee up in their hands, lest thou dash thy foot against a stone.

Thou shalt tread upon the lion and adder: the young lion and the dragon shalt thou trample under feet.

Because he hath set his love upon me, therefore will I deliver him: I will set him on high, because he hath known my name.

He shall call upon me, and I will answer him: I will be with him in trouble; I will deliver him, and honour him.

With long life will I satisfy him, and shew him my salvation.
PSALM 91 (KJV)

• • •

Hear me when I call, O God of my righteousness: thou hast enlarged me when I was in distress; have mercy upon me, and hear my prayer.

O ye sons of men, how long will ye turn my glory into shame? how long will ye love vanity, and seek after leasing? Selah.

But know that the LORD hath set apart him that is godly for himself: the LORD will hear when I call unto him.

Stand in awe, and sin not: commune with your own heart upon your bed, and be still. Selah.

Offer the sacrifices of righteousness, and put your trust in the LORD.

There be many that say, Who will shew us any good? LORD, lift thou up the light of thy countenance upon us.

Thou hast put gladness in my heart, more than in the time that their corn and their wine increased.

I will both lay me down in peace, and sleep: for thou, LORD, only makest me dwell in safety.
PSALM 4 (KJV)

Acknowledgments

Thanks to Almighty God for your enduring love, for the gift of your Son, and for the anointing, presence, and understanding of the power of the Holy Spirit.

There are so many people that I want, need, and should thank that have not only actively participated in the creation of this book, but also through their teachings and inspiration have helped to influence the message behind the pearls: "You can and should *expect to win*." I know that I cannot thank everyone by name, so please accept my heartfelt appreciation and gratitude if your name does not appear here. There are a few people, however, who I must thank here, who were instrumental to getting the pearls to print:

To my agent, Barbara Lowenstein, thank you for believing in this project from our first meeting and for having the foresight to arrange that magical breakfast in Times Square where you introduced me to Cherise Davis Fisher. I have learned a great deal from you.

To Cherise Davis Fisher, thank you for being an incredible editor. Honesty, directness, empathy, and responsiveness are all, as I have learned, hallmarks of an A-list editor who can produce high-impact outcomes. I thank you for taking the risk, leading the charge, and understanding the need for the pearls.

To the Hudson Street Press/Plume family, and in particular to Luke Dempsey, Marie Coolman, Liz Keenan, and Cristi Hall: Thank you for your focus, responsiveness, and outstanding execution. Luke, your enthusiasm from the start was infectious and affirming, and Marie, Liz, and Cristi, your marketing and publicity skills are unparalleled.

To Kellie Tabron, what can I say? I could not have produced this project without you. Your brilliance as a writer, calm spirit, consistent patience, outstanding research, tenacious focus, and commitment to deadlines (smile) made this journey not only easier than I could ever have imagined, but simply a pleasure. Shall we do it again?

To the *Essence* Magazine family, particularly Susan Taylor, Angela Burt-Murray, and Michelle Ebanks, thanks for creating the Women Who Are Shaping the World Conference and providing an incredible platform to discuss "Carla's Pearls." You are the ultimate "value-add" for all women and particularly women of color, as you are in a class by yourself. To Linda Villarosa and Terrie Williams, thanks for your incredible advice and for the push to get moving on this project.

To Morgan Stanley, particularly John Mack, Tom Nides, Jean-Marie McFadden, Marilyn Booker, and MaryClare Delaney, thank you for being incredibly supportive of Carla Harris, the banker and Carla Harris, the woman. And to a firm that has and continues to provide me with a career that has brought me lessons and experiences beyond what I could ever have imagined walking out of Harvard Business School twenty-one years ago, I say thank you.

To Hope Knight, Sharon Hall, Cynthia Hickman—mentors extraordinaire? consiglieri? truth tellers? What can I say? As the Master-Card slogan says, "You are Priceless." Thank you for your comments on the book, your advice, the late night/before dawn conversations, your shoulders, and your ears.

To Richard Parsons, William Lewis, Reginald Van Lee, Robert Scott, Vikram Pandit, John Havens, Richard Kauffman, Matthew DeSalvo, Joseph Perella, Jim Gantsoudes, and Gerald Adolph, thank you for being some of the men, albeit unbeknownst to some of you, who showed me "how to get it done."

To Richard Parsons, Terrie Williams, Sharon Hall, Ann Fudge, Sharon Epperson, Deborah Elam, and Kim Nelson, thanks for your willingness review of *Expect to Win* and for your incredible quotes and feedback.

To my mentees and those who have come out to hear me talk

about Carla's Pearls, thank you for trusting me as your mentor and for your honest questions and concerns, and for sharing your issues, for it was your quest for "how to navigate" and "how to get through it" that was the driving motivation to get the pearls from the podium to publication.

To my nanny, Betty Milstead, Audrey Smith and family, the Franklin family, all of my aunts, uncles, and cousins, Sherryl James, Dr. Vietta Johnson, Charlene Jackson, Judith Aidoo, Vernita Williams, Karla Elrod, Scott Cooper, Tanya Odom, Kathy Frazier, Caren Sharpe, Argie Johnson, Damon Caldwell, William Wright, Joe Tyler, Yolanda Joe, the Super family, Lisa Genova, Harry Van Dyke, Mark Howell and the Mark Howell Singers, the St. Charles Gospelites and my St. Charles family, Wanda Pierce, Marie Girardeau, Pamela Sanders, Paula and CJ Farrell, Ron and Beverly Riddick, Samantha Dulaney, Gemma and Pedro Morales, Lia Sanfilippo, Selene Martinez, Wilma Dore and Merault Almonor, and Eric Harris and family, thank you for your steadfast love, support, and encouragement, and the thousands of "attagirls" that you have given me throughout my life and this journey. You are "the wind beneath my wings."

To Monsignor Wallace A. Harris, a true Shepard, messenger of the Word, thank you for your love and confidence, and for teaching me that no matter what, God is indeed good, ALL OF THE TIME and ALL OF THE TIME, GOD IS GOOD.

To my grandmother, Mrs. Emma J. Smith, you were the first businesswoman I ever met and you taught me to be a fearless, focused, hard driving, no-nonsense decision maker. Thanks, Grandmama!

To my wonderful partner and husband, Victor Franklin, thank you for your love, support, tolerance, and temperance. You are a true partner and my number one!

Finally to my dad, John Harris, without you, mama, and God, I would not be here. Thank you for teaching me one of my most valued lessons, "the Street is just like the streets," and for being the man that you are. I have learned a lot from you.

About the Author

Currently a managing director for Morgan Stanley, Carla A. Harris spent over seventeen years of her career in capital markets and executed the IPOs for UPS, Martha Stewart Living Omnimedia, and Redback, as well as the $3.2 billion common stock transaction for Immunex, one of the largest biotechnology common stock offerings in U.S. history. Harris has been the recipient of numerous honors and awards, including *Black Enterprise*'s "75 Most Powerful Blacks on Wall Street" (2006), *Black Enterprise*'s "50 Most Powerful Women in Business" (2006), *Fortune*'s "The Most Influential List" (2005), *Ebony Magazine*'s "15 Corporate Women at the Top" (2004), *Essence Magazine*'s list of "The 50 Women Who Are Shaping the World" (2003), and *Fortune*'s list of "The 50 Most Powerful Black Executives in America" (2002).